Reaping The
Revenue Code

Reaping The Revenue Code

Why We Need Sensible Tax Reform For Sustainable Agriculture

Justin R. Ward
F. Kaid Benfield
Anne E. Kinsinger

*Natural Resources
Defense Council*

New York, NY

Production, design and typography: Wayne E. Nail
Cover design: Sue Burruss
Printing: Doyle Printing and Offset Company, Landover, Maryland

Natural Resources Defense Council, Inc.
122 East 42nd Street
New York, NY 10168

1350 New York Avenue, N.W.
Washington, DC 20005

90 New Montgomery
San Francisco, CA 94105

Portions of this book have appeared in different form in *The Harvard
Environmental Law Review*, the *Journal of Agricultural Taxation and Law* and
the *Virginia Environmental Law Journal*.

Table of Contents

Preface i

1: Introduction 1

2: The Tax Reform Act—Stemming the
   Revenue Code's Contribution to Surplus 7
   The Crop Surplus Problem 7
   The Impact of 1986 Tax Reform 10
       Capital Investment 11
       "Passive" Farming 14
       Deductions That Boost Surplus 15
   The Future of Tax Shelter Farming 16

3: Unfinished Business—Ending Tax Subsidies
   for Poor Stewardship 23
   The Environmental Costs of Poor Stewardship 23
       Sodbusting 23
       Swampbusting 26
       Excessive Irrigation 27
   The Emergence of Public Conservation Policy 31
   The Contradictory Impact of the Tax Code 33
       Cash Accounting 33
       Accelerated Depreciation 34
       Water Depletion Allowance 36
       Fertilizer and Lime Deduction 36
   Completing the Task of Tax Reform 37

4: Farm Chemicals—An Excise Tax to Fund
   Research and Education 47
   The Rising Tide of Farm Chemicals 47
   The Alternative of Low-Input Agriculture 50
   Obstacles to Low-Input Farming 52
   A Modest Excise Tax to Fund Research
   and Education 55

5: **The Rural Landscape—Proposals for
   Farmland Taxation** 65
   The Importance of Prime Farmland 65
   State Tax Laws and Their Shortcomings 70
   Recommendations for Improving State Laws 74
   Federal Law and Policy 76

6: **Conservation Easements—New Applications
   for Sustainable Agriculture** 85
   Conservation Easements Generally 85
   Taxation of Conservation Easements 87
   Agricultural Applications 89
      Farmland Protection 89
      Retirement of Eroding Cropland 91
      Groundwater Protection 92
   Proposals for Strengthening Tax Benefits
   for Easements 93
      Monitoring and Enforcement of Section 170(h) . 94
      The Problem of Appreciated Value 95
      Estate and Gift Taxation 96
   The Need for Complementary Incentives 98
      Easements for Farm Credit Relief 98
      Direct Purchase of Easements 99

7: **Private Forestry—Taxing the Tree Farm** 105
   The Untapped Potential of Private Forestry 105
   Environmental Benefits 106
   Environmental Risks 108
   Barriers to Private Forestry 110
   Public Forestry Programs 111
   The Impact of the Tax Code 113
   A More Realistic Approach 118
   Conditions for Federal Benefits 120

8: **Conclusion—A Tax Agenda for Conservation** 131

Appendix A: **Passive Investment Loss Limitations** . . . 135

Appendix B: **Depreciation of Capital Investments** . . . 137

Appendix C: **The Limited Reach of the Food
Security Act** 141

Preface

American agriculture evokes many pleasant, pastoral images–from expansive wheat fields and rows of corn to grassy plains and valleys where livestock graze. The nation is learning, however, that behind these images the condition of the rural landscape is dependent upon complex social, political, economic and environmental factors. In fact, the extent and nature of many farming practices are influenced as much by policymakers in Washington, D.C., and state capitals as by farmers in the field or consumers in the market.

Unfortunately, although modern American farming practices have resulted in huge amounts–indeed, a surplus–of food and fiber, this nation's success in agriculture has been far from unqualified. Ample evidence now confirms that our rural environment is suffering serious degradation from the massive farming system it supports. Increased runoff carrying cropland sediment to streams and rivers, toxic chemical contamination of soils, aquifers and farm products, and drainage of critical wetland habitat for surplus crop production are among the most disturbing trends within American agriculture.

Moreover, during much of the 1980s, the economic plight of debt-ridden farmers dominated American headlines. So did the severe drought conditions of 1988. The problems that plague American farming are particularly evident in the Midwest, the nation's breadbasket.

NRDC's Project on Agricultural Conservation and Tax Policy was conceived during deliberations on the 1985 federal Food Security Act. The landmark "sodbuster" and "swampbuster" provisions of that statute struck for the first time at federal programs that had previously rewarded abusive cropping of highly erodible lands and wetlands. NRDC was a strong supporter of these reforms, and has worked since their enactment to assure their full and strict enforcement.

Our interest in the Internal Revenue Code was sparked by a belief that the powerful incentives and disincentives in tax law should complement rather than subvert the Food Security Act's conservation mandate. This book examines how the federal government and the states can structure tax policy to achieve consistency with natural resource programs and promote a healthy rural economy and environment.

We must caution that the book is not primarily about the nuts and bolts of the tax code, a complex subject about which we have learned a great deal but on which we do not profess to be expert. Certainly, we do not intend to render professional legal or tax accounting advice. Rather, we have approached our subject as students concerned about public policy and the environment, and we hope that like-minded readers will find something of interest within these chapters.

As the title suggests, our research has led us to believe that too many agricultural investors for too long have reaped tax benefits rather than sensible harvests based on reasonable farming practices. While the ideas in this volume are surely in need of refinement, we hope to stimulate discussion that will lead to a fair set of reforms to promote sustainable, not destructive, agriculture.

The many sources of support and advice for this project could form a chapter unto themselves. We are particularly grateful for the tax law expertise furnished by Victor Thuronyi of the State University of New York School of Law at Buffalo. We are also indebted to Deanne Kloepfer, whose editorial skills helped us join a series of interim monographs into a unified whole.

Within the Natural Resources Defense Council, our special thanks go to Laura Teachout and Wayne Nail, who took charge of producing the book. Over the course of the project, several members of NRDC's Agriculture Program staff contributed helpful research; these included Caleb Corkery, Marci DuPraw, Richard Hardt and Tom Kuhnle.

We received valuable advice from more sources than it is possible to list. We nevertheless wish to mention particularly the constructive comments and information offered by Chuck Benbrook, Frederick Cubbage, Paul Ellefson, Peter Emerson, Neil Harl, Chuck Hassebrook, Ralph Heimlich, Ferd Hoefner, William Lockeretz, Peggy Miller, Ron Plain, Sandra Schlicker, William Siegal, Richard Wiles and Caroline Woodwell.

Accountability for all views expressed in this book, of course, rests with the authors.

Generous grants provided by The Joyce Foundation gave this study its start and its continuity. In addition, the project would not have been possible without additional generous grants from the Mary Reynolds Babcock Foundation, the Jessie Smith Noyes Foundation and the Wallace Genetic Foundation. Our deepest appreciation goes to these sources of support.

Justin R. Ward
F. Kaid Benfield
Anne E. Kinsinger
March 1989

About the Authors

Justin R. Ward is Senior Project Associate for NRDC's Agriculture Program in Washington, D.C. He received the American Farmland Trust's 1988 Agricultural Conservation Award for National Public Education. He is a graduate of the University of Montana at Missoula and the Hubert H. Humphrey Institute of Public Affairs at the University of Minnesota.

F. Kaid Benfield is a Senior Attorney in NRDC's Washington office. Since graduating from Georgetown University Law Center in 1972, he has specialized in federal administrative and environmental law and since 1981 has been Director of NRDC's Agriculture Program.

Anne E. Kinsinger was a Project Associate for the NRDC Agriculture Program from 1985-1987. She holds a Bachelor's degree from the University of California at Davis and currently is pursuing graduate studies at the Yale University School of Forestry and Environmental Studies.

1

Introduction

Agriculture is this country's largest industry. The food and fiber production system contributed 16.6 percent of the gross national product in 1986. Nearly one-fifth of the nation's private sector work force is engaged in growing, processing and distributing farm products.[1]

Moreover, the industry's productivity is on the rise: during the last four decades, American farmers have doubled their production volume and efficiency.[2] By current estimates, one farmer in the United States meets the food and fiber needs of 74 people.[3]

The implications for the American environment are profound. A vast amount of the nation's 2.3 billion-acre land base is used for crop, livestock and forest production. Indeed, more than 90 percent of the country's privately owned land is devoted to farming. In the 12 states of the midwestern heartland, agriculture is an especially significant pursuit; more than 880,000 farms–40 percent of the national total–are located in this region.[4]

Within American agriculture, tax law has had an enormous, if largely unappreciated, impact on whether land is farmed, for what commodities and with what intensity. While various tax incentives undoubtedly have contributed positively to the high volume of domestic agricultural production, they also have been a source of economic disruption and environmental damage. Until recently, however, policy makers have paid little attention to these impacts.

Change has begun. On October 22, 1986, then-President Reagan signed the Tax Reform Act, describing the measure as "less a reform than a revolution." The Act shifted a substantial portion of the federal tax burden from individuals to corporations, reduced or cancelled the tax liabilities of millions of low income individuals and eliminated many longstanding deductions and credits in exchange for generally lower tax rates and fewer tax rate categories.[5] Fairness and simplicity were common rhetorical themes during the arduous reform process, although public opinion remains divided over whether these aims were achieved.

A notable, if little publicized, departure from past tax policy debates arose during the writing of the 1986 legislation. It centered on the need to make the tax code consistent with the requirements of environmental protection; for the first time, citizens concerned about the environment had a voice in an arena previously regarded as outside the mainstream of environmental policy.[6] When the dust settled, the conservation agenda had been furthered in some important respects in the Tax Reform Act.

This beneficial result did not come about by accident but, rather, from years of attention drawn to the issue by diverse expert sources. In particular, the Environmental Defense Fund (EDF) in 1985 produced an important study, with comprehensive recommendations, on environmental tax reform.[7] Some of EDF's ideas, and others, were advanced by Senator John Chafee (R-RI) in legislative proposals and hearings.[8] In addition, a number of environmental organizations banded together in an umbrella group, the Environment and Economy Project, and met regularly throughout the reform process to develop strategy and share information.

A similar foundation had been laid for reform proposals important to agriculture. In a landmark 1980 report, "A Time to Choose," the U.S. Department of Agriculture (USDA) found that tax law was a major determinant of the structure of the nation's farming industry. In addition, noted agricultural economists such as Iowa State University's Neil Harl, Washington State University's Richard Dunford and USDA's Ralph Heimlich had demonstrated in numerous publications that tax policy is often just as influential as agriculture policy in determining what happens to the nation's farmers and rural landscape. Others whose ideas became prominent in the 1986 debate include Chuck Hassebrook of the Center for Rural Affairs and Bill Galston of the Roosevelt Center for American Policy Studies.

Because the Tax Reform Act did so much to change the rules, this book devotes considerable discussion to that legislation and its aftermath. The Tax Reform Act is only part of the story, however, and the book also examines the relationship between taxation and a number of critical natural resource issues affecting rural America today.

Chapter 2 examines the pervasive problem of surplus crops and explains why the Tax Reform Act should ultimately prove beneficial to farmers and the rural environment by reducing overproduction. In a related vein, Chapter 3 assesses and proposes refinements to new tax code provisions favoring conservation of soil, water and wetlands.

Chapter 4 discusses deficiencies (notwithstanding some encouraging progress) in the federal commitment to sustainable farming research. The chapter makes the case for a modest excise tax to fund expanded research and development of agricultural systems that can reduce pesticide and fertilizer application.

Chapter 5 focuses on the need to protect prime farmland from permanent conversion to incompatible uses. States have relied heavily on tax incentives for this purpose, but most state laws need substantial refinement to do much good. In addition, the federal government needs to structure its affairs so as not to undercut good state programs for conserving productive farmland.

Chapter 6 explores promising, if largely untested, ways to protect agriculture and the environment through conservation easements. The Internal Revenue Code provides generous benefits for easement donation; these should be protected and augmented.

Chapter 7 looks at another kind of agriculture, sustained tree farming on private forestlands. A majority of this nation's commercial wood stocks rest on non-industrial private forests, and these lands represent the best source to meet rising demands for timber. Tax laws, as well as direct public assistance programs, should be framed to account for the economic risks associated with private forestry while providing appropriate environmental safeguards.

Chapter 8 recapitulates and synthesizes the major recommendations introduced in the earlier chapters. The recommendations are intended as fodder for enlightened tax and conservation reforms into the twenty-first century.

Chapter Notes

1. *See generally* USDA, *1988 Fact Book of Agriculture* (Misc. Pub. No. 1063) (July 1988).

2. USDA, *Economic Indicators of the Farm Sector: Production and Efficiency Statistics* 9, 75 (ECIFS 5-5) (Apr. 1985).

3. *Id.* at 62.

4. *1988 Fact Book of Agriculture, supra* note 1, at 136. The 12 states are North Dakota, South Dakota, Nebraska, Kansas, Iowa, Missouri, Minnesota, Wisconsin, Michigan, Illinois, Indiana and Ohio.

5. *See generally* H.R. Rep. No. 841, 99th Cong., 2d Sess. (Report of the Conference Committee on the Tax Reform Act of 1986).

6. *See* B. Blackwelder and P. Carlson, "Tax Reform as Environmental Policy," 72 *Sierra* 33-36 (Mar./Apr. 1987); "The Environment Gets a Break as Well," 8 *Discover* 13 (May 1987).

7. W. Brown, *Eliminating Tax Subsidies to Protect Critical Habitat for Endangered Species and Other Natural Areas* (Environmental Defense Fund) (Feb. 4, 1985.)

8. *See* S. 1839, 99th Cong., 1st Sess., 131 Cong. Rec. S.15,118-15,120 (Nov. 7, 1985).

2

The Tax Reform Act–Stemming the Revenue Code's Contribution to Surplus

"Surplus" production of farm commodities that go begging on national and foreign markets has been a fixture of American agriculture since the 1950s. By 1986, crop surplus had reached mammoth proportions as the nation's storehouses held an excess of nearly two billion bushels of wheat, four billion bushels of corn and five million bales of cotton.[1] Production declines brought on by the national drought in 1988 reduced surplus volumes significantly, but that situation was not typical of the past decade.

Historically, surplus production has been assisted mightily by several tax preferences that were repealed in the 1986 Tax Reform Act. This chapter examines the likely impact of that statute and considers the wisdom of options for its amendment.

The Crop Surplus Problem

A moderate amount of extra crop production can provide a useful buffer against periodic crop failures and wide swings in market prices and farmers' incomes. To this end, the federal government administers emergency stocks of certain basic commodities, such as the 147 million-bushel Food Security Wheat Reserve.

Beyond maintenance of emergency stocks, however, surplus is the bane of the farm economy. Farmers experience the brunt of the impact as commodity prices fall in response to the laws of supply and demand. During 1987, for example, when the national corn surplus averaged nearly four times its 1981 level,[2] inflation-adjusted corn prices hit rock bottom, dropping even below comparable prices of the Dust Bowl period in the 1930s.[3] Low crop prices contributed to widespread foreclosures on farm mortgages and to other manifestations of economic depression in the nation's agricultural heartland.

Ultimately, taxpayers are forced to foot the bill. Government support payments to stabilize farmers' incomes in periods of declining crop prices climbed from $4 billion in 1981 to more than $25 billion in 1986.[4] Additional surplus-related costs include federal payments to farmers for acreage diversions, totaling $1.6 billion in 1987, and storage costs for government-held stocks of grain, which reached $1.4 billion that same year. The Export Enhancement Program, which pays grain traders to liquidate American surpluses on world markets, cost the taxpaying public another $1.2 billion in 1988.[5]

Surplus crop production also presents serious problems for human health and natural resources. The Conservation Foundation recently estimated that growing just the surplus portion of the 1986 corn and wheat crops commanded 7.3 billion pounds of fertilizer and 110 million pounds of pesticides.[6] On the average, surplus production accounts for some 15 percent of fertilizer and pesticide use on farms across the nation.

Even storing surplus grain presents significant health hazards. Toxic pesticides are used extensively to fumigate grain stored in silos and elevators. A regulatory notice issued by the U.S. Environmental Protection Agency (EPA) in 1985 reported that "chemical fumigants as a group are known to be acutely toxic, and overexposure to fumigant vapors can cause serious acute illness or death."[7] The notice banned fumigants containing three pernicious chemical compounds—carbon tetrachloride, carbon disulfide, and ethylene dichloride.

EPA's action came in direct response to mounting evidence of the extreme hazards associated with those substances. Unfortunately, the ban came too late to ensure public health protection in parts of rural America. In 1986, inspectors found carbon tetrachloride in 10 private wells in close proximity to a grain storage facility in Yoder, Kansas.[8] In Hospers, Iowa, two wells near a grain elevator were found to be contaminated with the same fumigant.[9]

Several toxic fumigants have not yet been banned and, in fact, are still widely used. According to EPA, one key fumigant ingredient, methyl bromide, is California's second leading cause

Crop surpluses have occurred frequently in the United States over the past 40 years. Grain elevators in Fairfield, Washington *(above)*, could not accommodate the heavy yield of winter wheat during 1976, forcing temporary "storage" in the town's streets. *Photo by Earl R. Baker; courtesy of USDA Soil Conservation Service.*

of hospitalization from occupational exposure to pesticides, and the cause of 10 reported deaths in that state between 1982 and 1985.[10]

Surplus crop production also exacts a heavy toll from natural resources that are essential to sustainable agriculture. Where rainfall is limited, for example, surplus crops often require pumping of underground aquifers for irrigation.[11] Overproduction parallels the steady decline of groundwater levels under half the nation's irrigated cropland.[12] According to the latest comprehensive appraisal issued by USDA's Soil Conservation Service, much of the Great Plains and the Southwest will face severe water shortages by 2030 if current rates of groundwater depletion persist.[13]

Surplus crops also appropriate enormous quantities of rural land. Surplus volumes of corn, wheat, soybeans, cotton and rice commanded 127 million acres in 1987, nearly one-third of the nation's total acreage in crops during that year.[14]

A significant amount of the land involved is extremely prone to erosion. The Soil Conservation Service's latest national inventory estimates that nearly one-fifth of the cropland in Illinois, the leading state for corn production, is eroding at twice the rate of natural soil regeneration.[15] As Worldwatch President Lester Brown recently observed:

> Headlines during [the 1980s] have focused attention on a "world awash in grain" and on the depressed prices that have resulted. The real story, however, is not the surpluses but the soil losses incurred in producing them. The surpluses are a fleeting phenomenon, but the soil losses will have a lasting effect on land productivity.[16]

In sum, fragile rural lands are falling victim to abusive plowing and aquifer depletion, as described more fully in Chapter 3. Farm chemicals continue to pollute the environment and threaten public health (Chapter 4). These problems are disturbing in any context but should be regarded as intolerable when they produce a glut of crops that no one wants to buy.

The Impact of 1986 Tax Reform
While many factors including technology, crop price supports, trade policy and faulty international distribution systems contribute to crop surplus, the federal tax code has also been a major

force. Agriculture's longstanding tax-favored status has harbored significant opportunities for farm investors "to reduce or even eliminate tax liabilities on relatively large incomes" through tax shelter preferences offered by the Internal Revenue Code.[17]

Indeed, some analysts maintain that the entire socio-economic structure of the country's agricultural sector is an artifact of tax policy. A 1984 study prepared for the Joint Economic Committee of the U.S. Congress concluded that the Revenue Code:

1) exerted upward pressure on farmland prices;

2) helped concentrate farmland ownership by high-income farmers and nonfarmers;

3) encouraged the substitution of capital for labor;

4) supported growth trends in the number of very small farms and very large farms, at the expense of medium-sized farms;

5) reduced efficiency in farm activities through changes in management practices; and

6) increased supplies and lowered prices for some, and possibly all, farm commodities.[18]

In exchange for lower tax rates for most individuals, the Tax Reform Act of 1986 removed many of the deductions, credits and exclusions that had caused these distortions.[19] As one *Money* magazine report stated, "[T]he big tax benefits of farm investing were sent to the compost heap."[20] Key features of the landmark law—notably its treatment of capital investment, "passive" losses and production expense deductions—should help cure the revenue code's bias for overproduction.

Capital Investment. In 1962, Congress enacted the Investment Tax Credit in an effort "to jump-start the economy." Under the most recent version, taxpayers could offset their tax liability with credits up to 10 percent of their investments in depreciable capital assets. In agriculture, the benefit was available for tractors and other machinery, equipment such as land drainage tiles and buildings used for a single purpose such as livestock confinement.*

The Tax Reform Act repealed the Investment Tax Credit.[21] The House Ways and Means Committee report on tax reform explained the intent behind the repeal:

> The strategy that any particular business might choose as most promising-whether to employ more or less equipment or labor, adopt different management practices, alter marketing and purchasing procedures, and so on-is a matter ... best left to private decisionmaking, undistorted by large tax preferences which presume that one answer fits all cases.[22]

USDA economists predict that the absence of the Investment Tax Credit will bring about a general decline in agricultural investment over the next several years.[23] This should reduce the motivation to produce surplus, to the benefit of natural resources, environmental quality and the farm economy.**

Further stifling the Revenue Code's bias for overproduction, the 1986 reform ended preferential treatment of capital gains.[24] Under prior law, individual taxpayers could exclude from taxation 60 percent of income obtained from selling capital assets, if the assets had been held for at least six months. Corporations enjoyed similar benefits from a maximum capital gains tax rate that was substantially lower than the maximum rate for ordinary income. Within agriculture, these provisions yielded major tax

---

* In *Showdown at Gucci Gulch*, an excellent account of the 1986 tax reform, *Wall Street Journal* writers Jeffrey Birnbaum and Alan Murray observe that the Investment Tax Credit "became one of the biggest tax expenditures in the code, resulting in billions of dollars of lost revenue to the Treasury each year."

** To cushion the effects of repealing the Investment Tax Credit, the new law preserved an accelerated cost recovery system, enabling deduction of investment property over periods considerably shorter than the property's useful life (*see* Chapter 3 and Appendix B). As the Joint Committee on Taxation's *General Explanation of the Tax Reform Act* points out, this was intended to ensure that "investment incentives will remain high" by retaining "[a]n efficient capital cost recovery system ... essential to maintaining U.S. economic growth" (chapter note 31 at 98).

savings when applied to sales of land, depreciable buildings and equipment and some other assets such as orchards and certain livestock.

There is little doubt that the tax code, in combination with high inflation and bullish expectations for continued prosperity, drove rural land prices up in the 1970s. Writing in 1981, analysts for the National Agricultural Lands Study warned that "preferential tax treatments are capitalized into higher land prices."[25] In fact, the majority of economic returns on farm investment during the 1970s came from capital gains, principally from land ownership transactions.[26]

This was decidedly harmful to the rural environment as new acreage—much of it erosion prone or ecologically sensitive—was purchased, plowed for expanded annual crop production and resold in the 1970s. Speculators reaped the rewards of increased land values resulting not only from the general inflationary trend but also from the boost in property values obtained by converting pasture, range and forest to intensive crop production. These benefits were augmented by investors' ability to deduct all interest expenses related to financing the conversions.

Although short-term speculators gained, long-term farmers suffered. In the 1980s, when export markets dried up and commodity prices fell, land prices also plummeted. A 12 percent aggregate decline in farmland prices in 1985 represented the most precipitous drop since the depression era of the 1930s.[27] The downward spiral struck a particularly devastating blow to owners of farms where land prices had been driven to artificially high levels during the boom period of the 1970s. This made it even more difficult for farmers who had borrowed heavily against their inflated land collateral to obtain new credit and repay loans, thus adding another straw to the back of the well-publicized farm debt crisis of recent years.

In general, repeal of the capital gains preference should help mitigate dislocation from wide swings in farm markets. The rural economy is less apt to become "over-heated" in boom cycles, making farmers less susceptible to abrupt free falls during hard times.

More specifically, repeal of the capital gains differential should help deter speculative cultivation of fragile lands that, while often marginal for farming, are important for wildlife habitat and other ecological values. In addition, the Tax Reform Act reinforced its general repeal of the capital gains preference with language specifically proscribing capital gains treatment of income from sales of highly erodible land and wetlands converted to crop production.[28] Although this provision is largely symbolic at present, it could deter production of surplus commodities on fragile rural lands if, in the future, Congress raises tax rates for ordinary income or restores a general exclusion for capital gains.[29]

"Passive" Farming. The Tax Reform Act also instituted a major shift from prior law concerning losses from so-called "passive" investments. Specifically, losses from business activities in which the taxpayer does not materially participate may no longer be deducted without limitation but instead may offset only that taxable income realized from passive sources.[30]

The new passive loss restrictions were enacted to address widespread concern "that the tax system was unfair, and ... that tax is paid only by the naive and the unsophisticated."[31] The objective was to close shelters used primarily by wealthier persons to escape their equitable share of the tax burden.

Fairness was not the only issue. Congress also concluded that:

> The availability of tax benefits to shelter positive sources of income ... harmed the economy generally, by providing a non-economic return on capital for certain investments. This encouraged a flow of capital away from activities that provided a higher pre-tax economic return, thus retarding the growth of the sectors of the economy with the greatest potential for expansion.[32]

Consequently, the reform legislation sought to limit "further expansion of the tax shelter market" and thus to discourage the diversion of investment capital "from productive activities to those principally or exclusively serving tax avoidance goals."[33] In agriculture, the new rules should reduce tax shelter farming that has stimulated investment in crops and livestock irrespective of market supply and demand and has thereby promoted overproduction of farm commodities.

The new law, however, leaves ambiguous the critical definition of "material participation" in investments. It states only a general instruction that taxpayers must involve themselves "on a regular, continuous, and substantial basis."[34] As of early 1989, an extensive set of regulations on the subject was pending at the Internal Revenue Service. A more detailed discussion of the passive loss limitations may be found in Appendix A.

Deductions That Boost Surplus. Ordinarily, the tax code treats long-term investments as capital items that are excluded from annual deductions and accounted for only at the time of sale of the property. Prior to the Tax Reform Act, however, preferential exceptions were allowed for financial outlays in clearing land and undertaking soil and water conservation in connection with agricultural production.

The land clearing exception was repealed in 1986,[35] although a limited deduction remains for routine brush removal and related maintenance of fields already under cultivation. This eliminates an anachronism in the tax code that rewarded needless expansion of the nation's cropland base. During a two-year period in the mid-1970s, when the rural economy was booming, this nation's farmers spent approximately $1.5 billion to clear an estimated 11 million acres of land, often without soil conservation precautions.[36] The new reform should ensure that tax subsidies will no longer help finance such destructive practices.

Supplementing repeal of the land clearing deduction, the Tax Reform Act restricted annual deductions for soil and water conservation to those expenditures consistent with plans approved by the Soil Conservation Service or a "comparable agency." The Act also explicitly disqualifies the deduction of "conservation" expenses associated with the draining and filling of wetlands and the preparation of land for center pivot irrigation.[37]

Pursuant to the old Revenue Code, farmers could deduct without restriction conservation expenditures totaling up to one-fourth of their gross incomes from farming. Nationally, farmers claimed nearly $129 million in conservation deductions for the 1980 tax year alone, and the deduction was particularly popular in the Corn Belt and Southern Plains regions.[38]

Many of the practices that once qualified for this tax preference were capital investments primarily serving production enhancement rather than erosion control or water conservation. In fact, deductions were claimed for such dubious measures as stream diversion, wetland drainage and leveling of hills for irrigation installations. Widespread misapplication of the conservation deduction led USDA economists to conclude that the provision's outright repeal "would not have a serious adverse effect on efforts to promote soil erosion control on U.S. cropland."[39]

The new provision should end abuse of the conservation deduction but continue to reward the installation of soil- and water-saving practices for farmers seriously committed to conservation. This will particularly assist producers affected by the 1985 Food Security Act's conservation compliance provision, which sets a 1995 deadline for implementation of locally approved systems to protect highly erodible cropland.[40]

Lawmakers scaled back deductions for land clearing and conservation explicitly to address the issue of farm surplus. As staff for the Joint Committee on Taxation explained, "Congress was concerned that these provisions were contributing to an increase in the acreage under production, which in turn encouraged the overproduction of agricultural commodities."[41]

The Future of Tax Shelter Farming

By some accounts, agriculture was among the "losers" in tax reform. This assessment stems from modern farming's heavy reliance on capital investment and the reform legislation's removal of many investment tax preferences. This prospect was not lost on agribusiness: an advertisement from Continental Grain Company issued prior to the 1986 debate argued for reform in the opposite direction, urging that "more liberal investment tax credits, faster tax write-offs for plant and equipment, and putting U.S. companies on an equal tax footing with their foreign counterparts ... could be the start of a comeback for industry, our economy and our farmers."[42]

Naysayers notwithstanding, most farmers eventually should face lower tax liability and increased profit under the new tax law.[43] Increased neutrality in the Revenue Code will correct biases that have fueled overproduction, distorted markets for land and farm products and created general instability in the rural economy. The Revenue Code certainly will be more consistent with acreage set-asides and related farm policy designed to promote supply and demand equilibrium. As noted agricultural economist Neil R. Harl has concluded:

> The message ... is clear: agriculture does not need the tax-induced investment that would increase aggregate output. Increased output brings a disproportionate drop in price and in profitability. The attack on tax shelters in the Tax Reform Act of 1986 is indeed justified.[44]

There is no guarantee, however, that the 1986 reforms will be given time to work. Almost immediately, no fewer than 213 tax bills were introduced in the Senate and another 536 were introduced in the House of Representatives in the next Congress.[45] Some agricultural preferences eliminated by tax reform—although none of the major provisions discussed in this chapter—were reinstated as part of "technical corrections" tax legislation enacted in 1988.* Others undoubtedly will resurface in future Congresses.

Of importance to farm surplus and natural resources, several pieces of recently proposed legislation would create a new Investment Tax Credit. One bill introduced just a few months after the Tax Reform Act was enacted would have restored the tax credit specifically for farming.[46] USDA economists have predicted additional "strident efforts" to reinstate the tax credit by lawmakers attempting to stem declining investments in agriculture.[47] This concern may be well founded; Congress has modified the Investment Tax Credit on four occasions since 1962.

A return to preferential tax rates for capital gains is also possible. Former President Reagan recommended such a change in his 1988 State of the Union address, acknowledging that the 1986 reform "did much to remove provisions that inhibit

---

* For example, the 1988 amendments eliminated a so-called "heifer tax" by revising the Tax Reform Act's repeal of deductions for "preproductive period costs." Under current law, farmers may once again expense rather than capitalize the purchase of orchard trees or expenditures on livestock to be raised for slaughter.

economic prosperity" but terming reduced capital gains taxation "the most important piece of unfinished business."[48] President Bush echoed this sentiment during his 1988 campaign and will likely press for capital gains breaks during his first term of office.[49] The proposal finds considerable support among advocates of "supply side" economics, who argue that reinstatement of a capital gains preference would spur savings and investment and ultimately boost tax revenues.[50]

This position is not universally held, however. A recent study by the Congressional Budget Office (CBO) projected that setting the maximum capital gains rate at 15 percent would cause declines ranging from $4 billion to $8 billion in annual revenue.[51] The CBO also has disagreed with the Bush and Reagan administrations on whether the 1986 tax reform as a whole has helped or hindered efforts to balance the budget. Whereas recent Treasury Department estimates suggest the 1986 reform package overall has exacerbated the federal deficit, conflicting figures from the CBO continue to reflect the opposite.[52]

Certainly, to the extent reinstatement of capital gains treatment or other preferences would add to the federal deficit, the farm economy would suffer. Throughout the farm crisis of the 1980s, the deficit acted as a major cause of persistently high interest rates that elevated farmers' operating costs while driving down their net incomes and land values.[53] Many economists regard deficit reduction as the "most important thing our policy-makers can do for farmers."[54]

Notwithstanding the calls for retrenchment, Congress should resist reinstatement of the Investment Tax Credit, the capital gains preference and other major benefits repealed in 1986. The economic and environmental costs of widespread tax shelter farming are simply too great to justify a return to the previous policies.

Chapter Notes

1.   D. Martinez, "Surplus Stocks Decline Sharply," 6 *Farmline* 4 (June 1988).

2.   *Id.*

3.   Telephone conversation with M. Ray Waggoner, USDA⸴ Agricultural Stabilization and Conservation Service (July 13, 1988).

4.   The Conservation Foundation, *Agriculture and the Environment in a Changing World Economy* 5 (1986).

5.   Data on program costs furnished by M. Ray Waggoner and Richard Pazdalski, USDA Agricultural Stabilization and Conservation Service, Information Division, July 13, 1988.

6.   The Conservation Foundation, *supra* note 4, at 32.

7.   U.S. Environmental Protection Agency, Regulatory Status of Grain Fumigants, 50 Fed. Reg. 38,092 (Sept. 19, 1985).

8.   E. Lawless and F. Hopkins, *Pesticide Contamination of Ground Water From Point-source, Agriculture-related Activities* 18 (Midwest Research Institute) (Sept. 30, 1987).

9.   Iowa Department of Water, Air and Waste Management, Report of Investigation (Hospers, Iowa) (May 31, 1984).

10.   U.S. Environmental Protection Agency, *Guidance for the Reregistration of Pesticide Products Containing Methyl Bromide as the Active Ingredient* 7 (Office of Pesticides and Toxic Substances) (Aug. 1986).

11.   A former deputy administrator of USDA's Economic Research Service has urged an end to public subsidies for irrigation development for the production of surplus crops. *See* M. Cotner, "Waterbusting: Irrigation Investment Aggravates Commodity Surpluses," 42 *Journal of Soil and Water Conservation* 337 (Sept.-Oct. 1987). *See also* Chapter 3 *infra*.

12.   G. Sloggett, *Prospects for Groundwater Irrigation: Declining Levels and Rising Energy Costs* 8 (USDA-ERS Agricultural Economic Report No. 478) (Apr. 1982).

13.   USDA Soil Conservation Service, *The Second RCA Appraisal: Review Draft* 7-1 (July-Aug. 1987). The "water resource" regions for which irrigation water

shortages are projected include Texas-Gulf, Rio Grande, Lower Colorado, and Great Basin.

14.   Food and Agricultural Policy Research Institute, "Comparative Analysis of Selected Policy Options for U.S. Agriculture," Figure 6 (Feb. 1987).

15.   USDA Soil Conservation Service, *Basic Statistics: 1982 National Resources Inventory* 47 (1987).

16.   L. Brown, "Breakthrough on Soil Erosion," 1 *World Watch* 20 (May-June 1988).

17.   R. Dunford, *The Effects of Federal Income Tax Policy on U.S. Agriculture* S. Prt. No. 273, 98th Cong., 2d Sess. 18 (Joint Economic Committee) (1984).

18.   *Id.* at 29.

19.   Tax Reform Act of 1986, Pub. L. No. 99-514, 100 Stat. 2085 (amending provisions of 26 U.S.C.) [hereinafter TRA].

20.   R. Eisenberg, "How City Slickers Can Live Off the Land," 17 *Money* 138 (Jan. 1988).

21.   TRA §211 (amending I.R.C. §49 (1982)).

22.   House Committee on Ways and Means, *Report on the Tax Reform Act of 1985*, H.R. Rep. No. 426, 99th Cong., 1st Sess. 146 (1985).

23.   R. Conway *et al.*, "Economic Consequences of Tax Reform on Agricultural Investment," iii, 37, 40 (USDA-ERS Technical Bulletin No. 1741) (Feb. 1988). This analysis projects additional modest increments of reduced agricultural investment from less accelerated schedules for depreciating some capital assets and from reduced income tax rates.

24.   TRA §§301-302, 311 (amending I.R.C. §§ 1(j), 1202, 1201).

25.   M. Caughlin and J. Noble, "Implications of Federal Tax Provisions for Agricultural Land Availability," in *Agricultural Land Availability* 482 (Senate Agriculture Committee Print) (July 1981).

26.   J. Lee, *Farm Sector Financial Problems: Another Perspective* 11 (USDA-ERS Agriculture Information Bulletin No. 499) (1986).

27.   *See* USDA Economic Research Service, *Agricultural Land Values and Markets* 1,3 (No. CD-90) (Aug. 1985). In many parts of rural America, farmland values did not begin to stabilize until 1987 and 1988.

28.   TRA §403 (creating I.R.C. §1257). The proscription applies to land converted after March 1, 1986.

29.   This was one conclusion of a recent government study on wetlands. *See* U.S. Department of the Interior, *The Impact of Federal Programs on Wetlands: Volume I* 30-31 (Oct. 1988). This report notes that the capital gains proscription does not extend to sales of wetlands converted to purposes other than annual crop production.

30.   TRA §§501-502 (creating I.R.C. §469).

31.   Joint Committee on Taxation, *General Explanation of the Tax Reform Act* 210 (May 4, 1987).

32.   *Id.* at 212.

33.   *Id.* at 210.

34.   Senate Committee on Finance, *Report on the Tax Reform Act of 1986*, S. Rep. No. 313, 99th Cong., 2d Sess. 732 (1986). Commenting on the TRA, experts in agricultural taxation have remarked that "[t]he meaning of material participation becomes more obscure each time the Congress uses it in the Code." *See* J. O'Byrne and C. Davenport, *Farm Income Tax Manual: 1987 Supplement to Ninth Edition* 351 (1988).

35.   TRA §402 (repealing I.R.C. §182). For each year claimed, the deduction was limited to $5,000 or 25 percent of taxable income from farming, whichever was less.

36.   *See* D. Lewis and T. McDonald, *Improving U.S. Farmland* 1 (USDA-ERS Agricultural Information Bulletin No. 482) (1984).

37.   TRA §401 (amending I.R.C. §175).

38.   W. Anderson and N. Bills, "Soil Conservation and Tax Policy," 41 *Journal of Soil and Water Conservation* 226 (July-Aug. 1986).

39.   *Id.* at 228.

40.   Food Security Act of 1985, Pub. L. No. 99-198, §1212(a)(2), 99 Stat. 1354, 1506-1507, 16 U.S.C. §3812(a)(2).

41.   *General Explanation of the Tax Reform Act of 1986, supra* note 31, at 188.

42.   Continental Grain Company advertisement *reprinted in* Environmental Policy Institute, *What Agribusiness Thinks ...* App. B (Aug. 1985).

43.   *See* C. Rossi, *Estimating the Effects of Tax Reform on Farm Sole Proprietorships* (USDA-ERS Staff Report No. AGES880913) (Dec. 1988).

44.   N. Harl, "The Future of Agricultural Credit," in *American Agricultural Law Association: Ninth Annual Conference* 9-20 (University of Missouri) (1988).

45.   A. Swardson, "Lawmakers Clamor Anew for Tax Breaks," *The Washington Post* H1 (Apr. 17, 1988).

46.   S. 455, 100th Cong., 1st. Sess., 133 Cong. Rec. S. 1647-1649 (Feb. 4, 1987).

47.   Conway *et al.*, *supra* note 23, at 40.

48.   President's 1988 Legislative and Administrative Message to the Congress 18 (Jan. 25, 1988).

49.   P. Blustein, "Bush likely to Push for Capital-Gains Tax Cut," *The Washington Post* D1 (Oct. 27, 1988).

50.   *See* D. Russakoff, "Tax Cut for Capital Gains Called Peril to '86 Law, Boon to Wealthy," *The Washington Post* A11 (Jan. 26, 1988).

51.   U.S. Congressional Budget Office, *How Capital Gains Tax Rates Affect Revenue: The Historical Evidence* 66 (Mar. 1988).

52.   *See* P. Blustein, "Tax Change to Worsen U.S. Deficit," *The Washington Post* A1 (Jan 13, 1989); P. Blustein, "CBO: Law Isn't Adding to Deficit," *The Washington Post* D1 (Jan 14, 1989).

53.   *Taxes and Agriculture: Hearing Before the Joint Economic Committee*, 98th Cong., 2d Sess. 49-50, 59 (statement of Dr. Neil E. Harl, Professor of Economics, Iowa State University) (1984).

54.   W. Galston, *A Tough Row to Hoe: The 1985 Farm Bill and Beyond* 39 (Roosevelt Center for American Policy Studies) (1985).

3

Unfinished Business–Ending Tax Subsidies for Poor Stewardship

In recent decades, American agriculture has pressed a vast amount of marginal and ecologically sensitive rural land into service. The nation's cropland base now encompasses an enormous fragile acreage that once existed as forests, native prairies or natural wetlands.

Such poor stewardship has been aided by a number of hidden subsidies in the tax code. These conflict with sound federal and state policy for conservation. Recommendations presented in this chapter are designed to eliminate environmentally harmful inconsistencies in public programs.

The Environmental Costs of Poor Stewardship

Indiscriminate crop production can have profoundly negative impacts on the rural landscape. Some of the most serious derive from the plowing of highly crodible land, drainage of wetlands and excessive pumping of irrigation water for crop production. Each of these practices presents its own set of problems.

Sodbusting. In the last century, pioneers recognized the damages of sodbusting to the undeveloped Great Plains; renowned western artist Charles M. Russell decried the destruction of extensive fields where the plow had turned prairie topsoil "grass-side down." The Dust Bowl of the 1930s stands as a particularly infamous manifestation of wind erosion in rural America.

Had he been alive this decade, Russell would have found continuing destruction on the landscapes he loved. During the winter of 1986-87, 1.5 million acres of Great Plains cropland suffered damage from wind erosion.[1] Nationally, in a 1982 inventory, the federal Soil Conservation Service found 86 million acres of cropland eroding at more than twice nondegradation thresholds. Forty-one percent of these lands were being damaged primarily by wind, 59 percent primarily by water runoff.[2]

Despite longstanding conservation programs administered by USDA, and some particularly important progress over the last three years, much of the land currently enlisted for annual rowcrops remains sorely in need of soil retention treatment, if not outright retirement. Approximately 118 million acres of cropland, only one-third of which are adequately protected against excessive erosion, are currently classified as "highly erodible" under farm legislation.[3] This amount is roughly the combined size of Wisconsin, Illinois, Indiana and Ohio, and represents more than one-fourth of the estimated 421 million acres currently in the cropland base. The largest regional concentrations of highly erodible cropland are found in the Corn Belt, the Rocky Mountain states and the Great Plains.[4]

In fact, largely as a consequence of cropland erosion, agriculture ranks as this nation's leading cause of "nonpoint source" water pollution.[5] Soils removed from farm fields by rainfall or irrigation water fill streams, lakes, bays and estuaries with sediment as well as chemical nutrients and toxins. The cumulative impact on society is enormous; a 1985 study by the Conservation Foundation estimated an annual cost in the neighborhood of $2.2 billion in damages from cropland runoff to domestic and industrial water use, fishing, boating, swimming, water storage facilities, navigation, flood control, irrigation, wastewater treatment and electric power generating facilities.[6]

Moreover, land stripped of topsoil may also suffer productivity reductions.[7] For example, soybean yields on severely eroded piedmont soils in the Southeast have been 50 percent less than yields on soils experiencing moderate erosion rates.[8] Over the long run, excessive erosion may jeopardize the world's food supply, in spite of the complacency that tends to arise from recent crop surplus and technological advances.

The prospects are troubling indeed if, as in the recent past, large amounts of new land are claimed for high-intensity agriculture. USDA estimates that nearly 227 million acres of highly erodible land that is now protected as pasture, range and forest have potential for being plowed and planted to erosion-

Runoff from erosion-prone fields often carries sediment into nearby streams, as occurred in 1983 in the rolling Palouse hills of eastern Washington *(above). Photo by Jim McCabe; courtesy of USDA Soil Conservation Service.*

prone rowcrops such as corn, wheat, soybeans and cotton.[9] Much of this land susceptible to destructive "sodbusting" is in the Great Plains, the Rocky Mountain states and the Appalachian Mountains.[10]

Swampbusting. Wetlands destruction is another environmental problem of the first order. Characterized by wet (hydric) soil and plants that thrive in perpetually moist conditions (hydrophytes), wetlands provide vital wildlife habitat, biologic diversity and clean water.

Once ubiquitous, natural wetlands are now scare. From the mid-1950s to the mid-1970s, an estimated 87 percent of all the wetlands lost nationally were lost to agriculture.[11] In some midwestern states, including Iowa, Michigan, Minnesota, Nebraska and Wisconsin, agricultural drainage of wetlands, or "swampbusting," has been instrumental in the virtual elimination of the pre-settlement natural wetlands base.[12]

In addition, more than five million acres of still-existing natural wetlands have high or medium potential for conversion to cropland.[13] Half this land is located in the southeastern states of Alabama, Arkansas, Florida, Georgia, Kentucky, Louisiana, Mississippi, North Carolina, South Carolina, Tennessee, Virginia and West Virginia.[14] Another one-third is found in the Corn Belt, the Great Lake states and the Northern Plains.[15]

Perhaps the principal harm caused by swampbusting is the loss of critical habitat for wildlife. For example, the black bear, white-tailed deer, bobcat and alligator all find refuge in the dense shrub cover of coastal North Carolina's pocosin wetlands.[16] These are among the areas most threatened by agricultural conversion.[17] Intensive crop production already has had an adverse impact on ducks, geese and other migratory birds that depend on the prairie pothole wetlands of the Dakotas and Minnesota, regarded as "North America's most valuable waterfowl breeding ground."[18]

Undisturbed wetlands are also valuable as natural agents of water pollution abatement, flood control, groundwater replenishment and mitigation of shoreline erosion.[19] There is even some evidence that wetlands contribute to local and global climatic stability.[20] These important functions are sacrificed when wetlands are drained and planted to crops.

Excessive irrigation. Irrigation fuels a large segment of this nation's farm production machine. In arid places, irrigation permits the raising of crops where farming would otherwise be impossible. In semi-arid zones, irrigation enables farmers to grow crops continuously on fields that, under nonirrigated "dryland" systems would have to be idled periodically for moisture retention and erosion control.[21]

Even in humid areas, irrigation provides insurance against extended periods of drought. Most farmers who irrigate experience significantly higher crop yields and enjoy greater versatility in the kinds of commodities they can raise.

Describing the proliferation in Nebraska of center pivot sprinklers, natural resource author James AuCoin has observed:

> ... the center pivot adapts well to coarse-textured and sandy soils, bringing irrigation to land that previously could not be watered. Heavy flushes of water under traditional ditch irrigation would be sucked up by coarse or sandy soil, drawing the water below the root zone before the plants could absorb it. Traditionally confined to grazing, sandy and coarse soils are now being turned into cornfields.[22]

Since the 1950s, the center pivot technology has dramatically changed the social and physical landscapes of the Nebraska Sandhills, a region where much of the land has a high potential for soil erosion and other properties that make it unfit for sustained rowcrop production.[23]

Rapid irrigation expansion in recent decades has occurred in the Southeast, the Great Lakes states and in the Corn Belt, where the amount of irrigated land increased by approximately 60 percent from 1974 to 1982.[24] In a five-state area in the heart of the Corn Belt (Illinois, Iowa, Indiana, Ohio and Missouri), the irrigated farmland base grew from just 16,000 acres in 1949 to more than 800,000 acres in 1982.[25] While this trend likely will endure in the East as more rowcrop farmers enlist irrigation to supplement natural precipitation, a slumping farm economy has brought a recent downward trend in irrigation across the rest of the nation, where total irrigated acreage declined from 1978 to 1982.[26] Nevertheless, a 1986 federal survey of irrigation practices showed that roughly half of the irrigated cropland in the United States is devoted to the production of cotton, rice, grain sorghum, barley, soybeans and tobacco—all crops in surplus.[27]

Future predictions are highly speculative, with recent USDA projections for irrigated acreage in the year 2030 ranging from 20 million acres nationally under a "low stress" scenario to more than 68 million acres (roughly 40 percent higher than the 1982 total) under a "high stress" scenario that couples prosperous commodity markets with extensive environmental degradation.[28] These estimates do not account for new demand for irrigation that may be brought on by probable climate shifts caused by the global warming trend.[29]

Whatever the future, current irrigation practices are causing dangerously rapid depletion of aquifers.[30] Since the recharge process can be excruciatingly slow, depletion is akin to "mining" a nonrenewable resource. USDA researchers writing in 1986 reported groundwater mining on 14 million acres, constituting nearly half of all cropland irrigated from underground sources in Arizona, Arkansas, California, Colorado, Florida, Idaho, Kansas, Nebraska, New Mexico, Oklahoma and Texas.[31*]

Depletion is particularly acute in the enormous Ogallala Aquifer underlying portions of Colorado, Kansas, Nebraska, New Mexico, Oklahoma, South Dakota, Texas and Wyoming.[32] Environmental writer Dick Russell has succinctly described the current situation in that region:

> For centuries the Ogallala has flowed, seemingly inexhaustibly, beneath 225,000 square miles of the middle Great Plains. Water mined from its depths supports one-fifth of the irrigated cropland in the United States. Today, irrigators are pumping that water fourteen times faster than it can be replenished. Even though only 8 percent of the Ogallala lies beneath the state of Kansas, it provides irrigation water for over two million acres of land in twenty-four western [Kansas] counties, more than 75 percent of the state's irrigated land. Now, in many parts of that

---

* A recent USDA yearbook (*see* chapter note 30) points out that approximately 40 percent of irrigation water is drawn from aquifers. The proportion is much higher in regions with scarce surface water supplies; around 80 percent of irrigation water in the Great Plains, for instance, comes from underground deposits.

In 1982, a hydra-matic center pivot irrigation system covered a quarter section of land in this southwestern Nebraska cornfield. *Photo by Jim McCabe; courtesy of USDA Soil Conservation Service.*

region, the water level is down 40 percent from only twenty years ago, dangerously depleted in some places, seriously affecting river and stream flow in others.[33]

Charles Little, a noted author in agriculture and the environment, noted in a more graphic characterization that "for every gallon of water pumped out, only a teacup is restored by the natural processes of aquifer recharge."[34]

Current trends in groundwater mining could lead to serious economic dislocation. Iowa State University's Center for Agricultural and Rural Development recently projected that depletion of the Ogallala would reduce aggregate farm income more than $58 million annually by the turn of the century, even assuming moderate levels of agricultural exports and low energy prices.[35] As for the southern reaches of the Ogallala, groundwater shortages will by some estimates cause a 50 percent decline in the amount of land irrigated in the Texas High Plains by the year 2020.[36]

The social and environmental costs of excessive irrigation are largely preventable. Oklahoma State University economist James Osborn informed Congress in 1984 that, through more precise measurement of the moisture needs of crop plants, "[W]e can produce the same yields of crops in the high plains of Texas for a third less water."[37] Echoing similar sentiment, Resources for the Future economist Kenneth Frederick has noted that, "[I]f water is applied only when it will be used most effectively by the plant, higher yields with less water may be possible."[38]

The benefits of such conservation are being made more available by recent advances in the scheduling of irrigation. For example, electronic data networks give farmers computer access to up-to-the-minute weather information that helps them know when to irrigate their crops most efficiently.[39] A computer program used in Wisconsin to monitor soil moisture levels has been beneficial in conserving irrigation water and reducing the leaching of pesticides and fertilizers to groundwater.[40]

In addition, very encouraging findings have emerged from field studies involving compact, inexpensive electronic devices called gypsum blocks. This conservation strategy has been described by INFORM, a nonprofit research organization based in New York:

> Farmers ... use gypsum blocks to manage irrigations by installing them at several locations and depths in a field's crop-root zone. They read the blocks weekly or twice weekly to see whether they are irrigating unevenly and/or too frequently. Then, by experimenting over one or two seasons with practices intended to correct these problems, farmers learn which adjustments reduce their water use, cut energy and water costs and improve yields. They conduct these tests on small field sections so they can observe the impact of changes on yields before deciding which practices should be extended to entire fields...

> Sometimes the gains from using the method can be spectacular: An INFORM test on one strip of a 160-acre alfalfa field indicated that by using about 30% less water on the entire field the farmer could have earned $20,000 or more in higher hay yields alone.[41]

There are many other encouraging developments in irrigation technology. One is surge irrigation, in which water is sent down field furrows in pulses regulated to serve the exact moisture requirements of crops.[42] Another promising but underused method is drip irrigation, based on the application of small quantities of water transported through tubes to soil immediately surrounding individual plants. Drip is particularly well-suited to the cultivation of orchard crops in arid zones. Favorable conservation results have also been obtained with a highly efficient sprinkler system that uses very low pressure to feed water to crops through hoses that extend from elevated pipes.[43]

The Emergence of Public Conservation Policy

Myriad public policies have contributed to the rise of intensive crop production involving sensitive lands and limited water supplies. Primarily, before the Food Security Act of 1985, widespread federal price supports for farm commodities rewarded abusive sodbusting and swampbusting. The government also furnishes direct subsidies through artificially low water prices charged to irrigators who are served by Bureau of Reclamation projects in 17 western states.[44] A dramatic example is found in California's Central Valley, where large-scale growers of grains and cotton reap enormous benefits from irrigation water prices far below market value.[45] Other irrigation assistance is supplied through the Soil Conservation Service's small watershed development program.

Lingering problems notwithstanding, the legislative and administrative response to conservation needs in the 1980s has been impressive. Most notable has been Title XII of the 1985 Food Security Act,[46] which withholds federal farm program benefits from producers who are not conservation-minded stewards of the land.

Specifically, the statute precludes sodbusters and swampbusters from receiving federal commodity price support payments, income subsidies, subsidized crop insurance and low-interest loans from USDA's Farmers Home Administration.[47] A number of reasonable exemptions are provided, including one for producers who follow approved erosion control plans when they plow highly erodible fields.[48]

A leading objective of these provisions was the achievement of consistency across federal programs. Through the sodbuster restrictions, Congress cured an anomaly in which USDA had invested approximately $1 billion annually on soil and water conservation[49] while simultaneously abetting erosion problems through commodity program assistance. Similarly, the swampbuster provision mitigated conflicts between subsidies for agricultural conversion of wetlands and federal initiatives to protect wetlands.

An example of the latter is USDA's "water bank" program, under which farmers receive federal compensation for protecting wetlands under 10-year contracts.[50]

In addition, the Food Security Act contains language, although not specific sanctions or incentives, encouraging "dry land farming" as a method to achieve the national policy objective of energy and water conservation.[51] In approving this amendment to the Soil Conservation and Domestic Allotment Act (16 U.S.C. § 590g(a)), the Senate Agriculture Committee voiced its concern "with the vast expansion of irrigated cropland recently and the impact this expansion has had upon available water supplies and surplus crop production."[52] The Act thus follows USDA's 1982 national program under the Soil and Water Resources Conservation Act (Pub. L. 95-192), which also lists improved irrigation efficiency and water management as long-term conservation objectives.[53]

The Food Security Act's remedial provisions were reinforced by the 1986 Tax Reform Act, in which Congress explicitly repealed capital gains preferences for income generated by the sale of sodbusted and swampbusted land and restricted some deductions that had rewarded poor stewardship. These changes are noted above in Chapter 2.

State governments have also responded to the need for conservation. In Wisconsin and several other midwestern states, for example, legislatures have adopted "T by 2000" programs that affirm a commitment to achieve tolerable erosion rates by the turn of the century.

Some state initiatives aim to balance irrigation development with maintenance of water supply and quality. Among the 11 states with the largest areas of agriculture-related aquifer decline (Arizona, Arkansas, California, Colorado, Florida, Idaho, Kansas, Nebraska, New Mexico, Oklahoma and Texas), only Arkansas and California have yet to impose restrictions on groundwater use in irrigation.[54] Arizona has enacted the most stringent state law, which prohibits new irrigation in areas with critical groundwater supply problems.[55] A new statute in Illinois allows local Soil and Water Conservation Districts to restrict irrigation when there is evidence of "substantial drops in groundwater levels."[56]

The Contradictory Impact of the Tax Code

Despite these clear articulations of conservation policy, and despite some progress in the Tax Reform Act, tax subsidies for sodbusting, swampbusting, excessive irrigation and farm chemical use continue to reside in the unrestricted availability of four significant benefits, described below.

Cash Accounting. As a general matter, the Internal Revenue Code requires businesses that maintain inventories to compute taxes using the accrual method of accounting.[57] Taxpayers using this method may generally "report income when it is earned, claim deductions when expenses are incurred, and as nearly as possible recognize taxable income only for the taxable period for which it relates."[58]

The business of farming involves the maintenance of product inventories. However, most farms are covered by exemptions from the general rule on accrual accounting.

Specifically, the law exempts most individual farmers as well as corporations with gross annual receipts of $1 million or less. These taxpayers may use cash accounting and, thus, may expense in a given tax year financial outlays for such necessities as seeds, fuel, crop insurance premiums, pesticides and fertilizers used for production of crops harvested and sold during a subsequent tax year.[59] This can prove advantageous in a good year, enabling farmers to offset surplus income by spending to stock up on future supplies prior to the year's conclusion. Many farmers use cash accounting as a means of "income averaging" to reduce wide fluctuations in annual taxable income.[60]*

Recognizing the subsidy inherent in cash accounting, the Tax Reform Act of 1986 denied this option to farm syndicates and other agricultural operations designed primarily for tax shelter purposes.[61] In addition, for agricultural taxpayers who still may use cash accounting, the Act limited annual deductions for

---

* An optional "crop" method is available under which all crop production expenses, including seed or seedlings, must be deducted in the year the income from the crop is received. A "hybrid" method of accounting, combining aspects of the cash and accrual methods, is another option available to individual farmers.

prepaid supplies (such as feed, seed and fertilizer) to 50 percent of other deductible farming expenses paid during the tax year in which the supplies are purchased but not consumed.[62] These reforms should help reduce incentives for overproduction as well as for the indiscriminate conversion of fragile lands to agriculture. Nevertheless, the special benefits of cash accounting remain lucrative for many agricultural producers, including poor stewards.

Accelerated depreciation. In the aftermath of the 1986 Tax Reform Act, the most important Revenue Code provisions currently rewarding capital investment are those governing deductions for depreciation. In general, taxpayers may write off losses for the declining market value of investment property under somewhat artificial rules designed to encourage economic expansion. These benefits were generally preserved in the Tax Reform Act of 1986.

For the agricultural investor, the tax code's Accelerated Cost Recovery System allows deduction of the full cost of depreciable property over periods of time considerably shorter than the property's useful life.[63] Farm investors may write off investments for property ranging from tractors and sprinkler systems over just seven years and may deduct the expenses of ditch excavation, water well drilling and various other land manipulations over just 15 years.*

Taxpayers may elect to depreciate their property in equal annual increments under "straight line" schedules. It is usually advantageous, however, to claim disproportionately large write-offs in the early years of the recovery period using a "150 percent declining balance" method. Section 179 of the Revenue Code supplements these benefits with a deduction that allows a taxpayer claiming a total of $200,000 or less in capital investment during the tax year to expense an amount up to $10,000.[64]

A detailed description of accelerated depreciation and section 179 deductions may be found in Appendix B. In general, these

---

* The "technical corrections" tax bill enacted in 1988 extended the depreciation period for livestock confinement buildings and other single-purpose agricultural structures from seven years to 10 years (*see* Pub. L. No. 100-647, §6027).

Table 1

Recovering the Cost of a $90,000 Combine
Under Alternative Depreciation Schedules

	150 percent declining ACRS/ 7 yr. recovery w/ §179 expensing		Straight line ACRS/ 7 yr. recovery w/ §179 expensing		Non-accelerated Straight line/12 yr. recovery	
Year	Deduction	Present Value Tax Savings*	Deduction	Present Value Tax Savings*	Deduction	Present Value Tax Savings*
1	$18,572	$4,727	$15,713	$4,000	$3,707	$ 944
2	15,307	3,542	11,429	2,645	7,417	1,716
3	12,027	2,532	11,429	2,404	7,417	1,560
4	9,798	1,879	11,429	2,186	7,417	1,418
5	9,798	1,704	11,429	1,987	7,417	1,289
6	9,799	1,550	11,429	1,806	7,417	1,172
7	9,799	1,407	11,429	1,642	7,417	1,066
8	4,900	641	5,713	746	7,417	969
9	0	0	0	0	7,417	881
10	0	0	0	0	7,417	801
11	0	0	0	0	7,417	728
12	0	0	0	0	7,417	662
13	0	0	0	0	3,706	301
TOTAL	$90,000	$17,982	$90,000	$17,416	$89,000	$13,507

* This assumes the investor is in the 28% income tax bracket. The nominal tax savings are thus 28% of the deductions. Using an assumed 10% after-tax discount rate, the formula for calculating the present value of the tax savings in each year is: $[0.28 \text{ (deduction)}] + (1.1)^n$ where n is the year of the recovery period. At a higher discount rate, the present value of ACRS tax savings would be higher relative to straight line depreciation. Conversely, a lower discount rate would produce a smaller present value differential.

benefits enable investors to enjoy tax savings far sooner than they would under schedules more reflective of the actual length of time their investments can be used to generate income. As illustrated in Table 1, a high-bracket taxpayer who buys a combine for $90,000 and elects accelerated depreciation and Section 179 deductions can write off the total investment over just seven years. It is likely, though, that the machine will remain in service for 12 years or longer. As a result, the present value of the tax subsidy is more than $4,400.

Such benefits may be particularly significant in the plowing, draining and irrigating of fragile rural land. Characterizing the conversion of wetlands to agriculture as "an extensive, high-cost venture," researchers at Duke University recently attributed the vast amount of wetland drainage in North Carolina to large corporations' wherewithal to make large initial capital outlays without realizing positive financial returns until several years later.[65] Like wetland drainage, irrigation is also a highly capital-intensive pursuit.[66]

Water Depletion Allowance.[67] Under current Internal Revenue Service rules, irrigation farmers may claim deductions under a water depletion allowance "when it can be demonstrated that the groundwater is being depleted and that the rate of recharge is so low that, once extracted, the groundwater is lost to the taxpayer and immediately succeeding generations."[68] The allowance derives from a 1965 federal court ruling that extended the cost depletion deductions associated with exhaustion of oil, gas and mineral reserves to farmers who draw irrigation water from the Ogallala Aquifer.[69]

The water depletion allowance permits farmers to deduct a theoretical financial loss for each foot of decline in a groundwater reserve underlying their property. The value per foot is calculated by dividing the total value of the groundwater–usually the initial price of the property attributable to the water–by the original depth of the aquifer.

For example, an individual may purchase a section of previously unirrigated cropland for $256,000 on the assumption that half the land's value derives from abundant reserves of groundwater. The theoretical cost of the water is thus $128,000. If the groundwater supply was 200 feet deep when the land was purchased, the depletion allowance subsequent to installation and operation of an irrigation system is calculated as follows:

$$\frac{original\ value\ of\ water\ =\ \$128,000}{original\ aquifer\ depth\ 200\ ft.} = \$640 \text{ per foot of decline.}$$

Thus, for every foot the aquifer declines each year, the farmer may deduct $640.

Fertilizer and Lime Deduction. Farmers may claim ordinary business expense deductions for fertilizer and lime applications that, in reality, are more akin to capital investments than operating costs. In particular, the deductions may be claimed for applications used to "enrich, neutralize or condition land" irrespective of whether productivity benefits extend–as they commonly do—over more than one year.[70] Without this special treatment, the tax code would require that such treatments be amortized, or written off in increments over the lifetime of the investment.*

This deduction effectively reduces the cost of purchased chemicals and indiscriminately rewards the frequent use of more fertilizer than is necessary to obtain desired crop yields. The result is often a subsidy of water pollution caused by the application of excessive nutrients that eventually are leached to groundwater or washed into surface streams and lakes.

The House Ways and Means Committee's version of tax reform in 1986 would have denied annual expense deductions for fertilizer and lime applications with multiyear effects. Although not adopted in the final legislation, the Committee's proposal was accompanied by the rationale that an unlimited fertilizer deduction "may be affecting prudent farming decisions adversely."[71]

Completing the Task of Tax Reform

It is time to finish the job begun in the 1986 Tax Reform Act. It is manifestly unreasonable for the Food Security Act and related policies to promote conservation, and for some provisions of the Internal Revenue Code to follow suit, while remaining tax subsidies reward unsustainable use of land and water. Appropriate reforms listed below would cure this contradiction.

First, the water depletion allowance should be repealed. Although not the most lucrative deduction claimed by irrigators, the allowance blatantly rewards environmental damage and contradicts federal and state policies for groundwater conservation. In addition, aquifer mining produces a cost to society at large, not just the irrigator. Repeal would appropriately require that at least a portion of these social costs be borne by those persons who are responsible.

---

* For tax purposes, the multi-year production enhancement from a fertilizer application is treated as an "intangible asset" subject to amortization over its lifetime. It is distinguished from tangible assets like machinery, whose cost is recovered through depreciation, and from improvements like land clearing, whose cost is "capitalized" or added to the taxpayer's "basis" (usually the initial purchase price) in the land.

The water depletion allowance not only frustrates public conservation policy, but its theoretical justification wrongly presumes an automatic reduction in the value of land or water rights as an aquifer declines. In fact, such reductions may be imaginary if the overlaying land in question is suited to an alternative use just as economically productive as irrigation farming. Moreover, as groundwater mining proceeds, the economic value of the remaining water generally goes up; this is unaccounted for in the current formula.

Second, expense deductions for fertilizer applications should be allowed only for fertilizer volumes likely to be assimilated by crop plants in a given year, and such deductions should be expressly disallowed for excess amounts that could leach to groundwater or cause gaseous emissions that exacerbate the atmospheric greenhouse effect. To substantiate a deduction, farmers should be required to document that the fertilizer applied does not exceed volumes specified by unbiased field test data on soil nutrients.[72]

By restricting deductions for fertilizer to amounts that legitimately can be considered necessary business expenses, the tax code would no longer tip the scales toward synthetic chemical use in excess of amounts needed to maintain crop yields. Farmers would have an incentive to engage in prudent fertilizer management by setting reasonable objectives, accounting for soil nutrients supplied by natural sources and adjusting the timing of chemical applications.[73] Improved water quality should result.

Third, so long as subsidies inherent in cash accounting, accelerated depreciation and expensing of capital assets exist in the revenue code, they should be restricted to practices that do not promote sodbusting, swampbusting or excessive irrigation development. This concept will need refinement, but a model can be found in legislation proposed in 1985 to deny special tax breaks, including accelerated depreciation and Section 179 expensing, for investments in the commercial development of "environmental zones." As conceived in the bill, these zones would have included sensitive areas such as endangered species habitat not governed by public ownership or other protective authority.[74]

To keep administrative confusion to a minimum, the denial of tax subsidies for environmentally destructive activity should be total with respect to the deduction in question. Accelerated cost recovery should not be allowed for a tractor used in sodbusting, for example, even if the tractor also may have been used for more benign purposes. This would obviate sticky prorating problems and be consistent with 1985 sodbuster and swampbuster sanctions that deny program benefits for all crops raised, not just those grown on unprotected highly erodible lands or natural wetlands.

To promote conservation, the repeal of subsidies should be structured so that, where highly erodible cropland is plowed, a farmer may retain eligibility for tax benefits by adopting effective practices to conserve topsoil. This, too, would parallel provisions of the Food Security Act.

Similarly, irrigators might retain eligibility for tax subsidies by adherence to compliance with state laws governing groundwater withdrawals and by adherence to such instruments as water conservation plans developed with technical assistance from the Soil Conservation Service.[75] Particularly strict standards should apply to the installation of irrigation systems on fields previously managed under a dryland regime.

Tax reforms aimed at sodbusting, swampbusting and excessive irrigation would provide a useful complement to the 1985 Food Security Act's conservation incentives which, unfortunately, are only as strong as the leverage inherent in USDA programs available to participating farmers. The Food Security Act thus constitutes an unreliable check—a "slender stick," in the words of two agricultural economists[76]—in the fight against future destructive cropping of highly erodible lands and wetlands. The risk will be especially great if Congress reduces funding for federal farm programs or if, as hoped, the 1990s bring substantial economic recovery in agriculture. A more complete discussion of the relationships between farm program participation and conservation incentives may be found in Appendix C.

Fortunately, removing tax subsidies for these activities need not be inordinately burdensome for farmers or for the Internal Revenue Service and other government agencies. Few compliance mechanisms would be required beyond those already established by USDA for administering existing conservation programs. These procedures typically involve only modest amounts of paperwork; farmers applying for program benefits, for example, routinely file short forms with USDA to certify their adherence to the sodbuster and swampbuster conditions.[77]

Under these proposals, even sodbusters, swampbusters and excessive irrigators would remain fully able to deduct all business expenses using the accrual method of accounting and to depreciate their capital investments using non-accelerated schedules. In this sense, the removal of tax subsidies stops short of imposing a tax penalty on these producers. Nevertheless, a strong argument can be made for legislation introduced in 1985 that would have denied *all* credits and deductions taken in connection with destructive cultivation of highly erodible lands and wetlands.[78] The inability to write off annual business expenses or depreciable investments would be an extremely powerful disincentive to reckless plowing and draining of fragile agricultural land.*

* There is ample precedent in the revenue code for denying business deductions for pursuits that frustrate public policy. In particular, section 162 disallows deductions for certain foreign advertising expenses, fines, bribes, lobbying, expenses of certain discriminatory health plans, or treble damages for antitrust violations.

Chapter Notes

1. "Gone With the Wind," 19 *High Country News* 6 (Mar. 30, 1987).

2. USDA Soil Conservation Service, *Basic Statistics: 1982 National Resources Inventory* 93, 99 (Statistical Bulletin No. 756 (Sept. 1987).

3. USDA, *Environmental Assessment for the Regulations Implementing the Highly Erodible Land Conservation Provisions of the Food Security Act of 1985* 21 (June 1986); USDA, *The Second RCA Appraisal: Review Draft* 4-18, 19 (July-Aug. 1987).

4. *Environmental Assessment for ... Highly Erodible Land Conservation...*, *supra* note 3, at 27.

5. U.S. Environmental Protection Agency, *Report to Congress: Nonpoint Source Pollution in the U.S.* 4 (Jan. 1984).

6. *See* E. Clark *et al.*, *Eroding Soils: The Off-Farm Impacts* xviii (The Conservation Foundation) (1985); *see also* M. Ribaudo, *Reducing Soil Erosion: Offsite Benefits* (USDA-ERS Agricultural Economic Report No. 561) (Sept. 1986).

7. *See, e.g.*, P. Crosson, "New Perspectives on Soil Conservation Policy," 39 *Journal of Soil and Water Conservation* 222-225 (July-Aug. 1984).

8. A. White, Jr. *et al.*, "Characterizing Productivity of Eroded Soils in the Southern Piedmont," in *Erosion and Soil Productivity* 94 (American Society of Agricultural Engineers) (Dec. 1984).

9. *Id.* at 24.

10. *Id.* at 27.

11. USDA, *Environmental Assessment for the Regulations Implementing the Wetland Conservation Provisions of the Food Security Act of 1985* 1 (June 1986).

12. J. Feirabend and J. Zelazny, *Status Report on Our Nation's Wetlands* 24, 28-31 (National Wildlife Federation) (Oct. 1987).

13. *Environmental Assessment for ... Wetland Conservation, supra* note 11, at 2.

14.   M. Brohan, "Wetlands to Farmlands: Curbing the Conversion," 7 *Farmline* 4 (Oct. 1986).

15.   *Id.*

16.   E. Maltby, *Waterlogged Wealth* 77 (Earthscan, 1986).

17.   R. Heimlich and L. Langner, *Swampbusting: Wetland Conversion and Farm Programs* 19, 22 (USDA-ERS Agricultural Economic Report No. 551) (Aug. 1986).

18.   *Id.* at 21.

19.   U.S. Office of Technology Assessment, *Wetlands: Their Use and Regulation* 43-52 (Mar. 1984).

20.   *Id.* at 60-61.

21.   *See* C. Little, *Green Fields Forever* 45 (1987).

22.   J. AuCoin, *Water in Nebraska: Use, Politics, Policies* 39, 41 (1984).

23.   *See generally* Center for Rural Affairs, "Beneath the Wheels of Fortune: The Economic and Environmental Impacts of Center Pivot Irrigation Development on Antelope County, Nebraska" (Mar. 1988).

24.   U.S. Department of Commerce, Bureau of Census, *1984 Farm and Ranch Irrigation Survey* 1 (Special Report Series Ag 84-SR-1) (June 1986). The increase was calculated from the South Atlantic, East South Central, East North Central and West North Central irrigation regions.

25.   USDA, *Agricultural Statistics* 374 (1985).

26.   A secondary cause of the interrupted growth trend is regional water shortages. Shortages have caused reduction in irrigated land in parts of the U.S. where the cost of pumping declining groundwater has become prohibitive. In Texas, for example, the amount of irrigated land dropped by 20 percent from 1978 to 1982. *The Second RCA Appraisal: Review Draft, supra* note 3, at 7-10, 7-11.

27.   *1984 Farm and Ranch Irrigation Survey, supra* note 24, at 2, 39-51.

28.   *Id.* at 12-17.

29.   *See* U.S. Environmental Protection Agency, *The Potential Effects of Global*

Climate Change on the United States 8-7 through 8-32 (Draft Report to Congress) (Oct. 1988).

30.   *See* H. Bouwer *et al.*, "Our Underground Water Supplies: The Sometimes Dry Facts," in *Using Our Natural Resources* 448-457 (USDA 1983 Yearbook of Agriculture).

31.   *See* G. Sloggett and C. Dickason, *Ground-Water Mining in the United States* (USDA-ERS Agricultural Economic Report No. 555) (Aug. 1986).

32.   Other areas experiencing serious irrigation-caused groundwater decline include the desert Southwest and parts of Florida, Arkansas and Idaho. D. Martinez, "Groundwater Irrigation: Where the Profits are Drying Up," 7 *Farmline* 4 (Nov. 1986).

33.   D. Russell, "Ogallala: Half Full or Half Empty?" 7 *The Amicus Journal* 13-14 (Fall 1985).

34.   C. Little, "The Great American Aquifer," 51 *Wilderness* 43 (Fall 1987).

35.   C. Short *et al.*, *Regional Impacts of Groundwater Mining From the Ogallala Aquifer with Increasing Energy Prices 1990 and 2000* 16, 95-96 (CARD Report 98) (Apr. 1981). Consistent with other findings, this study projects the most acute income losses to occur in the southern part of the Ogallala area. The study recommends a policy and research emphasis on conserving groundwater and energy instead of inter-basin transfers of surface water or other expensive and destructive means of supplying irrigation in the Great Plains.

36.   G. Sloggett, *Prospects for Ground-Water Irrigation: Declining Levels and Rising Energy Costs* iii (USDA-ERS Agricultural Economic Report No. 478) (Dec. 1981).

37.   *Ground Water Recharge in the High Plains States ... Hearings Before the Senate Subcommittee on Water and Power*, 98th Cong., 1st Sess. 37 (Statement of Dr. James Osborn, Chairman of the Department of Agricultural Economics, Oklahoma State University) (1984).

38.   K. Frederick, "Irrigation Under Stress," 91 *Resources* 4 (Spring 1988).

39.   Council for Agricultural Science and Technology, *Effective Use of Water in Irrigated Agriculture* 39-40 (Report No. 113) (June 1988).

40.   P. Holden, *Pesticides and Groundwater Quality: Issues and Problems in Four States* 76 (Board on Agriculture, National Research Council) (1986).

41.   G. Richardson and P. Mueller-Beilschmidt, *Winning With Water: Soil-Moisture Monitoring for Efficient Irrigation* 4 (INFORM) (1988).

42.   S. Scott, "Surge Irrigation Guide to be Published," 7 *Soil and Water Conservation News* 10 (July 1986).

43.   A. Wyatt and P. Bruno, "Ground-Water Conservation on the Texas High Plains," in *Using our Natural Resources, supra* note 30, at 460-461.

44.   A. Fox *et al., Production of Surplus Crops on Irrigated Land Served by the U.S. Bureau of Reclamation* viii-ix (USDA-ERS Staff Report No. AGES 831213) (Feb. 1984). Subsidized Bureau of Reclamation water is used on roughly one-fifth of all irrigated farmland nationally. *Id.* at 7. The states with the largest acreages of irrigated land served by Bureau of Reclamation water include California, Idaho, Washington and Colorado. *Id.* at 42.

45.   *See, e.g.,* E. LeVeen and L. King, *Turning Off the Tap on Federal Water Subsidies* 1-7, 46-49 (Natural Resources Defense Council and California Rural League Assistance Foundation) (Aug. 1985). Through the efforts of its Western Water Program, NRDC is promoting reduced agricultural consumption and pollution of water through the elimination of federal water subsidies.

46.   Food Security Act of 1985, Pub. L. No. 99-198, Title XII, 99 Stat. 1354, 1504-1518, 16 U.S.C. §3801 *et seq.*

47.   *Id.* §§1211-1213, 1221-1223.

48.   The Food Security Act exempts producers from its sodbuster sanctions if they comply with site-specific erosion control plans, usually developed with assistance from USDA's Soil Conservation Service, that are approved by locally elected conservation officials. The law also contains a "grandfather" exemption for highly erodible fields that were under the plow during any of the 1981-85 crop years; this exemption will expire in 1990 pursuant to "conservation compliance" language in the law.
    The swampbuster provision exempts crop production on natural wetlands whose agricultural conversion was "commenced" prior to enactment of the farm bill. Recognizing the impossibility of retaining ecosystem values under intensive cropland management, the law provides no exemption for swampbusters who practice soil and water conservation; an exemption was created, however, for activities with "minimal" impact on natural wetland characteristics.

49.   *See, e.g.,* USDA Soil Conservation Service, *FY 1988 Budget* (Jan. 5, 1987).

50.   *See Wetlands: Their Use and Regulation, supra* note 19, at 73-74.

51.   Food Security Act of 1985, *supra* note 46, §1253.

52.   S. Rep. No. 145, 99th Cong., 1st Sess. 303 (1985).

53. USDA, *A National Program for Soil and Water Conservation: 1982 Final Program Report and EIS* 1 (Sept. 1982).

54. Martinez, *supra* note 32, at 6.

55. D. Sheridan, *Desertification in the United States* 73-74 (U.S. Council on Environmental Quality) (1981).

56. "Small Farmers Win One in Illinois," 5 *The Land Stewardship Letter* 2 (Fall 1987).

57. U.S. Department of the Treasury, Internal Revenue Service, *Accounting Periods and Methods* 5 (IRS Publication 538) (Nov. 1986).

58. J. O'Byrne and C. Davenport, *Farm Income Tax Manual: Ninth Edition* 28 (1987).

59. U.S. Department of the Treasury, Internal Revenue Service, *Farmer's Tax Guide* 15, 7 (IRS Publication 225) (Oct. 1986). Outside agriculture, cash accounting is used by small businesses that do not maintain inventories.

60. *See* R. Dunford, "Farming the Tax Code," *Choices* 19 (Third Quarter, 1986).

61. Tax Reform Act of 1986, Pub. L. No. 99-514, §801, 100 Stat. 2085, 2345-2348 (amending I.R.C. §448) [hereinafter TRA].

62. *Id.* §404 (amending I.R.C. §464).

63. I.R.C. §§167, 168 [All I.R.C. citations are to the Code as amended by the TRA].

64. I.R.C. §179.

65. C. Richardson *et al.*, *Wetland Trends and Factors Influencing Wetland Use in North and South Carolina* 22 (U.S. Office of Technology Assessment and Duke University School of Forestry and Environmental Studies) (July 1982).

66. *See* G. Pavelis, *Natural Resource Capital Formation in American Agriculture: Irrigation, Drainage, and Conservation, 1855-1980* v (USDA-ERS Report No. AGES850725) (Sept. 1985). From 1976 through 1980, a period of rapidly expanding agricultural exports, the nations's farmers invested an average of $633 million annually for sprinkler irrigation equipment. These expenditures for sprinkler irrigation systems increased during the same period by an average of over 12 percent per year, far outpacing any other component of farm business capital.

67. I.R.C. §§611-613.

68. *Farmer's Tax Guide, supra* note 59, at 33; IRS Revenue Ruling 82-214.

69. *U.S.A. v. Shubert*, 347 F.2d 103 (5th Cir. 1965).

70. I.R.C. §180 (1988).

71. H.R. Rep. No. 426, 99th Cong., 1st Sess. 650 (Report of the Committee on Ways and Means on the Tax Reform Act of 1985).

72. Where possible, this documentation should come from state-certified test laboratories that rely on university research for conducting standard soil analysis and making recommendations for fertilizer use. Minnesota and Iowa have recently pioneered voluntary certification programs of this kind; other states will likely follow suit. *See* C. Cramer, "Finally ... Soil Tests You Can Trust," 10 *The New Farm* 12-16 (Sept.-Oct. 1988).

73. *See* D. Granatstein, *Reshaping the Bottom Line: On-Farm Strategies for a Sustainable Agriculture* 9-15 (Land Stewardship Project) (1988).

74. S. 1839, 99th Cong., 1st Sess. 131 Cong. Rec. S.15,118-15,120 (Nov. 7, 1985). *See also* W. Brown, *Eliminating Tax Subsidies to Protect Critical Habitat for Endangered Species and Other Natural Areas* (Environmental Defense Fund) (Feb. 4, 1985).

75. *See* USDA Soil Conservation Service, "Irrigation," in *SCS National Engineering Handbook* (Section 15).

76. K. Easter and M. Cotner, "Evaluation of Current Soil Conservation Strategies," in *Soil and Conservation Policies, Institutions and Incentives* 297 (Soil Conservation Society of America) (1982).

77. *See* USDA, Highly Erodible Land and Wetland Conservation; Interim Rule, 51 Fed. Reg. 23496-23514 (June 27, 1986) (to be codified at 7 C.F.R. Parts 12, 1940, 1941, 1943, 1945 and 1980).

78. S. 1786, 99th Cong., 1st Sess. 131 Cong. Rec. S.13913-15 (Oct. 23, 1985).

4

Farm Chemicals–An Excise Tax to Fund Research and Education

American agriculture depends heavily on chemicals to control crop pests and to fertilize soil. Pesticides and fertilizers have contributed to an era of outstanding farm productivity, but their intensive use is now endangering public health, polluting the nation's water supply and lowering farmers' profits.

Although sustainable crop production systems that enable farmers to reduce chemical use are being developed, lack of funding for research and education is a major obstacle to these systems' widespread acceptance. These issues are addressed in this chapter.

The Rising Tide of Farm Chemicals

Remarkable increases in the volume of American farm products have been accompanied by major increases in the application of agricultural chemicals (Figure 1). The nation's farmers now apply about 50 million tons of synthetic fertilizer to their fields each year, a level 15 times the annual amount used in the 1930s.[1] Pesticide use has also increased at a staggering pace; in 1966, American farmers applied approximately 300 million pounds of chemicals to control insects, weeds and plant diseases. By 1985, annual applications had risen to an estimated 860 million pounds.[2]

Some chemical application schedules are incredibly intensive. On southeastern cotton fields, it is not unusual for farmers to spray pesticides as often as 15 times per growing season.[3]

These trends pose serious problems for farmworkers, the segment of the population that suffers the greatest exposure to agricultural chemicals.[4] In 1986, the U.S. Environmental Protection Agency (EPA) limited use of the popular herbicide dinoseb on the basis of risks to agricultural workers, including birth

Figure 1

U.S. Agricultural Chemical Use
(fertilizers, pesticides and lime)

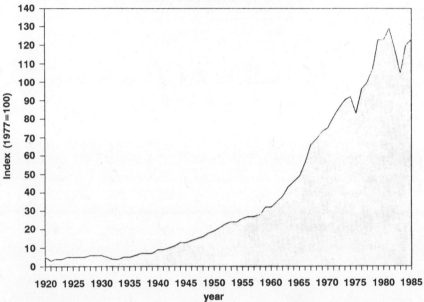

Source: USDA, *Fact Book of U.S. Agriculture* (Miscellaneous Publication No. 1063) (July 1988).

defects, male sterility and acute toxicity.[5] Similarly, recent National Cancer Institute studies on farmers in Kansas and Nebraska have shown an association between non-Hodgkin's lymphoma and the application of herbicides, particularly 2,4-D.[6]

A related and particularly insidious problem is groundwater contamination, rapidly emerging as one of the nation's foremost environmental concerns.[7] Although the magnitude of the problem has yet to be assessed fully, recent USDA reports indicate that 36 states have already documented instances of groundwater contamination with pesticides.[8] In addition, 30 states have recorded contamination with nitrates,[9] and a 1981 study found that 40 percent of all wells sampled in 14 Iowa counties exceeded the maximum level allowed by EPA.[10] A recent USDA study revealed that much of the groundwater underlying the East and Midwest may be polluted with pesticides, nitrates or both.[11]

Such contamination presents a significant health threat to rural areas, where 97 percent of all drinking water is obtained from the ground.[12] Indeed, more than 54 million Americans drink water from private wells and public groundwater supplies.[13]

With respect to pesticides, the substances most commonly detected in groundwater include atrazine, alachlor and aldicarb.[14] Atrazine is the most widely used herbicide applied to corn crops. Alachlor, currently the most widely used pesticide in the nation but banned in Canada, has been classified by EPA as a probable human carcinogen.[15] Aldicarb, considered the most acutely toxic pesticide in the world,[16] has been found in the groundwater of 15 states.[17]

Byproducts of synthetic fertilizers may also represent significant public health risks. Infant methemoglobinemia, a sometimes fatal disease more commonly called blue-baby syndrome, has been traced to fertilizer contamination of drinking water.[18]

In some circumstances, irrigation exacerbates the toxic chemical contamination of underground wells. This is partly because application of fertilizers and pesticides on irrigated cropland tends to be significantly higher than comparable application on dryland fields.[19] In Mason County, Illinois, for example, severe leaching of chemicals through soils resulted from the near doubling of fertilizer use with the advent of irrigated corn production.[20] Some of the nation's most serious nitrate pollution of groundwater occurs on irrigated agricultural lands in the West and Southeast, particularly in areas where vegetables such as potatoes are irrigated on sandy soils.[21]

The connection between irrigation and fertilizer contamination of aquifers in one midwestern farm state has been illustrated dramatically by James AuCoin:

> Nebraska's worst water quality problem is the pollution of its underground water supply with nitrates. In most areas where contamination is widespread, the cause is irrigation. Farmers can apply much more nitrogen fertilizer under irrigation than they ever could without irrigation because the additional water protects the plants form burning. The large amounts of nitrogen are washed through the soil and into the ground water supply.[22]

AuCoin noted further that the technology necessary to clean up groundwater supplies is "complicated and expensive," and that "some towns and cities, including Grand Island ... [Nebraska's] fourth largest city, have been forced to find new municipal well fields to escape nitrate contamination."[23]

The costs of protective measures also can be substantial. According to USDA economists, monitoring private wells for contaminants could cost households collectively as much as $1.3 billion every year.[24] For rural residents whose wells are contaminated, connecting to treated public water systems could cost each household an average of more than $12,000, not including service payments.[25]

In addition to health-related costs, buying chemicals has a major impact on farmers' pocketbooks. Expenditures for pesticides and fertilizers to grow corn in the Midwest in 1985 averaged $70 per acre, more than half of farmers' variable costs.[26] That same year, expenditures on chemicals to grow cotton in the Southeast averaged an astounding $134 per acre.[27]

Despite the rapid growth in pesticide use, significant crop losses remain attributable to insects, disease and weeds, including a cash-equivalent loss of $7 billion in a recent four-year period.[28] In part, pesticide failure is due to successful adaptation by pest species, many of which are now able to survive once-lethal doses of chemicals; as of 1984, about 600 pests were known to be resistant.[29] The National Research Council concluded in 1986 that "[t]he bright future projected for crop protection ... is now open to serious question" due to this pesticide resistance.[30]

A related problem is the emergence of secondary pest populations induced by the use of pesticides. These populations occur either when an eliminated pest is replaced by a new pest or when pesticide applications remove a natural predator and allow an existing second pest's population to rise to destructive levels.[31] A 1982 pest management text reported that in California, 24 of the state's 25 major crop pests are secondary populations whose growth is attributable to the use of pesticides.[32]

The Alternative of Low-Input Agriculture

There are promising alternative approaches that enable reduced chemical use in agricultural production. Often called "low-input," "organic" or "sustainable" agriculture, the alternatives include both systems that forgo synthetic pesticides and fertilizers altogether and those involving judicious applications of purchased chemicals.[33]

Many alternative practices are straightforward. For example, careful monitoring of insect populations can enable farmers to select and apply pesticides only when needed to prevent significant crop losses.[34] Similarly, more precise measurement of available soil nutrients can enable farmers to adjust the timing and volume of nitrogen fertilizer applications and thus mitigate nitrate leaching to groundwater.[35] Switching from continuous cultivation of a single crop to a more diversified operation can both reduce pest problems and enhance soil productivity.[36]

Apart from having become more sophisticated over the decades, there is nothing fundamentally new about low-input farming alternatives. Today's growing interest in these systems signals a renaissance that has been widely heralded in the press. Ward Sinclair, formerly an agriculture writer for *The Washington Post*, observed:

> Whether it is called sustainable, renewable, regenerative, organic, low-input or something else, it is essentially the same: an attempt to reduce or eliminate chemical pesticides and improve soil fertility by returning to the crop rotations that were common before the age of the chemical fertilizers.[37]

Modern use of the long-forgotten technology is often beneficial to farmers' financial interests as well as to conservation values. The many advantages of low-input agriculture were summarized in 1986 by the Congressional Office of Technology Assessment (OTA) as follows:

> [Y]ields per acre are generally equal to or only slightly less than those from conventional farming. Some organic farms have significantly higher-than-average yields. Second, production costs are lower by a high of 30 percent and an average of 12 percent, while energy inputs per unit produced are lower by 50 to 63 percent ... Third, soil erosion is significantly reduced through various cultivation practices ... If farmers shifted to organic production, farms would be more diverse biologically and economically, and the small farm could remain economically competitive and ensure diverse, competitive food production systems.[38]

The advantages of diversified farming operations are particularly significant. Alternatives to monoculture are integral to most low-input systems and often protect farmers against the financial pitfalls of hitching their fortunes to the market for a single commodity.

Another OTA study published 10 years ago estimated that, with available systems, American farmers could reduce aggregate pesticide use by as much as 75 percent from 1979 levels.[39] Projected to present-day circumstances, this would allow annual savings for a typical corn producer in the Midwest of approximately $14 per acre, more than one-tenth of average variable production costs.[40] Comparable reductions in the use of synthetic fertilizers and other farm chemicals could boost savings to more than $50 per acre, more than 40 percent of average variable costs.[41] The National Center for Appropriate Technology, a private, non-profit organization promoting sustainable agriculture, estimates that low-input systems could save American farmers an annual total of nearly $2 billion in fertilizer, $2 billion in pesticides and $3.3 billion in fuel costs.[42]

Although low-chemical farming practices typically require increased labor, the reduction in cash expenses is usually sufficient to compensate.[43] In 1984, for example, certain Texas cotton farmers using low-chemical pest control methods enjoyed net returns averaging $114 per acre more than their counterparts employing more conventional means.[44] Similarly, net returns for low-chemical almond growers in California have averaged $311 more per acre than those for other almond growers.[45]

Obstacles to Low-Input Farming

Despite these advantages, sustainable farming systems have not yet been adopted on a wide scale. Many farmers accustomed to intensive chemical use fear that changing their production systems will cause declining yields from insufficient soil fertility and high crop losses to pests. Some of this trepidation may be warranted, since it is common for yields to be somewhat lower in the early years of a phased transition to low-chemical systems. However, former yield levels are often regained in later years once the conversion is complete.[46]

Other factors behind the relatively low acceptance of sustainable methods include the additional time required for monitoring farming operations, skepticism toward unfamiliar technology, and consumer preference for uniform, unblemished farm products. Public policy also impedes a wide scale transition to sustainable agriculture in that federal price support payments for certain commodities reward maximum production and tend to require continuous planting of corn and other cash grain crops as a condition of eligibility. This places alternatives such as beneficial crop rotations at a competitive disadvantage, and encourages inefficient use of inputs, particularly nitrogen fertilizers, to attain high crop yields.

Many of the obstacles might be overcome with additional research to improve low-input systems and make them more widely available. As the Office of Technology Assessment concluded, "[A]lthough organic farming maintains soil quality better and reduces contamination of air, water, soil and the final food products, much research is needed to determine just why organic practices have this effect."[47] Research is particularly needed on issues such as the economics of the transition to low-input systems, more efficient management of crop nutrients and more effective use of biological methods of pest control.[48]

Some examples of the kind of research that would be helpful may be found in a number of pioneering local projects across the country. Researchers at the University of Nebraska, for instance, are conducting experiments designed to examine cropping systems that rotate corn with oats and nitrogen-rich legumes.[49] Studies at the University of North Carolina are focusing on crop yields and economic returns to evaluate some low-input systems in that state.[50]

Other promising research has been initiated by the Iowa State University Cooperative Extension Service, which in 1988 concluded the second year of an Integrated Farm Management Demonstration Project whose mission is "to implement the best innovative available crop production technology to protect soil and water resources, reduce energy consumption, and enhance farm profitability."[51] Similarly, the non-profit Land Stewardship Project's Model Farming Program is sponsoring additional applied research on sustainable production systems in southeastern Minnesota.[52] The University of California has initiated a program to fund low-input research and extension in that leading agricultural state.

Promising as they are, such local initiatives can have only limited influence and cannot approach the potential impact of federal research programs. More than half the agricultural research in this country is federally funded and is conducted primarily at land grant universities and their 58 affiliated agricultural experiment stations.[53] These institutions employ more than 7,000 scientists under a combined annual budget of more than $1.1 billion.[54]

In addition, USDA provides the principal education link between researchers and farmers with its Cooperative Extension Service, whose agents furnish technical information and assistance to farmers through county extension offices and farm visits. The Service's functions are supported annually by $995 million in government funds.[55]

Despite these considerable resources, USDA and the land grant universities historically have given little specific attention to low-input agricultural systems.[56] Farmers attempting to adopt sustainable systems that reduce purchased chemical inputs must engage in trial-and-error experiments on their own farms, without the benefit of the traditional research and extension network.[57]

Two new programs created in 1985 have strengthened federal support for sustainable agriculture. First, the Agricultural Productivity Act instructs USDA, in cooperation with universities and other private institutions, to conduct research and extension on farming systems that conserve energy and natural resources.[58] The intent is to emphasize on-farm research projects with immediate practical application for farmers.[59] This represents the first Congressional attempt to establish a unified low-chemical farming program at USDA.

Second, the Food Security Act created a program called Appropriate Technology Transfer to Rural Areas.[60] Managed by the National Center for Appropriate Technology, the program's objective is to "meet the critical need for information and assistance on low-chemical farming and community resource management."[61] Appropriate technology transfer seeks to assist farmers in lowering production costs by reducing use of fertilizers, fuel and pesticides.

These programs have demonstrated promising success even with modest budgets. For example, under the Agricultural Productivity Act, USDA has created a new Low-Input Sustainable Agriculture ("LISA") program administered by USDA's Cooperative State Research Service.[62] The program provides competitive grants to assist researchers in government and the private sector. The grants are overseen by regional panels of experts, including farmers, in sustainable agriculture.

Examples of projects funded in 1988 include: "substituting legumes for fallow in U.S. Great Plains wheat production;" "low-input ridge tillage systems for the Corn Belt;" and a videotape series for midwestern farmers on "making the conversion from conventional to sustainable agriculture."[63] The LISA initiative has garnered strong support from officials at USDA despite strenuous objections from the fertilizer industry.[64]

In addition, personnel for the appropriate technology transfer program have established a computer data base for ready access to research, have prepared technical data for distribution to farmers and have sponsored special education projects. Farmers and other citizens can now consult a team of agricultural specialists based in Memphis, Tennessee, through a toll-free telephone number.[65]

Although they represent important progress, the new low-input research and appropriate technology transfer programs remain the proverbial "drop in the bucket." For the Agricultural Productivity Act, Congress awarded just $3.9 million and in Fiscal Year 1988, less than one percent of USDA funding for all agricultural research. The appropriate technology transfer project received appropriations of just $750 thousand in Fiscal Year 1988, primarily to establish the Memphis facility. These levels amount to considerably less than one percent of the Extension Service's total budget.[66] The prospects do not appear great for a dramatic increase in support for either program.

A Modest Excise Tax to Fund Research and Education

Substantially greater funding for research and education on sustainable agriculture could be obtained through establishment of a federally administered trust fund, supported by a modest excise tax on pesticides and fertilizers. While administration of the trust need not bypass the annual appropriations process, Congress should be limited in appropriating money from the trust fund to uses that are consistent with its central purpose.

The Agricultural Productivity Act's programs should receive a substantial share of these appropriations. In particular, the program of competitive grants should be expanded to assist qualified researchers both inside and outside the traditional research system. Such grants allow peer review and encourage a wide variety of proposals that should increase the quality and diversity of sustainable agriculture research.

A fully funded program should continue to be overseen by expert panels, which should avoid making grants that would have little direct significance for low-input agriculture or would duplicate other research efforts.[67] In addition, grants should be oriented toward practical applications of low-input systems, sometimes called "adaptive" research, that can provide immediately useful models for farmers.[68]

The trust should also fund the extension work of the National Center for Appropriate Technology and the Extension Service to implement new low-input information centers and training programs and to undertake on-farm demonstrations, workshops and continuing education conferences.

Although funding for the trust would vary with fluctuations in product sales, a modest excise tax on pesticides and fertilizers should provide ample support for sustainable farming programs such as those described above. In 1985, American farmers spent more than $11.8 billion on pesticides, fertilizers and lime.[69] Just a half percent tax on this amount would provide $59 million annually, a one percent tax $118 million annually. At these rates, even a half percent tax would provide more than four times the 1988 appropriations to implement the Agricultural Productivity Act and Appropriate Technology Transfer.

The financial impact of the tax on farmers would be minor. For instance, for a person faced with the $70 per acre average annual fertilizer and pesticide outlays for midwestern corn production noted earlier, a half percent tax imposed upon retail sales of pesticides and fertilizers would raise expenditures by just 35 cents per planted acre. Some farmers might choose to offset this amount through a slight reduction in pesticide and fertilizer applications.[70] No significant effect on consumer prices would be likely.

Such a tax appropriately would benefit those persons who would pay it. Farm families, who suffer the most serious health risk from contamination of rural groundwater supplies and occupational exposure to toxic substances, would stand to gain the most from programs that help sustainable agriculture gain acceptance in the mainstream. Farmers would also reap whatever financial benefits result from wider availability of farming systems that produce satisfactory yields with lower production costs. Ultimately, consumers would also benefit, especially through reduced risk of chemical contamination in food products.[*]

Considerable precedent exists for the use of an excise tax to support a dedicated trust fund. Of the 34 excise taxes currently in place, fully half underwrite trusts that are earmarked for specific purposes.[71] A well-known example is the Highway Trust Fund tax imposed on goods purchased for highway use, such as motor fuels, tires, trucks, trailers and heavy-use vehicles.[72] The money collected for the trust, $15 billion in Fiscal Year 1986, directly benefits users, funding highway construction and maintenance.[73]

Similarly, the Airport and Airway Trust Fund is used for construction and maintenance of airport facilities; it is supported by taxes on airline tickets, domestic air cargo and fuel taxes on noncommercial aviation.[74] The airport and airway excise tax generated $2.4 billion in Fiscal Year 1986.[75]

A dedicated tax and trust fund for sustainable agriculture would not be troublesome to administer. In a system similar to that employed for other trust fund taxes, it could be collected from farmers by retailers at the time of purchase and transmitted periodically to the Internal Revenue Service.[76] At appropriate intervals, Congress could vote authority for expenditures in keeping with the trust's established purposes.

---

[*] This issue is elaborated in another 1989 study from NRDC titled *Intolerable Risk: Pesticides in Our Childrens' Food.*

Finally, a federal trust fund would be responsive to growing public support for taxes on pesticides and fertilizers to address groundwater contamination, pesticide resistance and related problems. Both the Worldwatch Institute and the World Resources Institute have called for a national pesticide tax to fund research.[77]

In addition, at the state level, a 1986 survey of Iowa residents revealed that a majority favored taxes on chemicals to help fund groundwater protection.[78] Subsequently, the Iowa legislature established a fund supported by pesticide registration fees, taxes on pesticide retail sales, pesticide dealer license fees and a fee amounting to 75 cents per ton on nitrogen fertilizers.[79] Revenues provide permanent funding for Iowa's Aldo Leopold Center for Sustainable Agriculture and support grants to counties to test for groundwater contamination and to plug abandoned wells.[80] Similarly, Wisconsin imposes a 20 cents per ton tax on fertilizers to fund groundwater protection and research.[81] Congress should tailor any new federal initiative to avoid duplication with these and other promising programs at the state level.[*]

---

[*] As noted by the Worldwatch Institute (chapter note 44), at least one other nation, Denmark, has adopted a national tax on farm chemicals. Revenues from a three percent tax on pesticide sales in Denmark provide funds for research and education to help achieve a 25 percent reduction in Danish pesticide use.

Chapter Notes

1.   U.S. Office of Technology Assessment, *Technology, Public Policy, and the Changing Structure of American Agriculture* 60 (Mar. 1986); USDA, *1984 Fact Book of U.S. Agriculture* 3 (USDA Miscellaneous Publication No. 1063) (Nov. 1983).

2.   U.S. Office of Technology Assessment, *Pest Management Strategies in Crop Protection, Volume I* 19 (Oct. 1979); U.S. Environmental Protection Agency, *Pesticide Industry Sales and Usage: 1985 Market Estimates* Table 3 (Economic Analysis Branch) (Sept. 1986).

3.   L. Suguiyama and G. Carlson, *Field Crop Pests: Farmers Report the Severity and Intensity* 12 (USDA-ERS, Agricultural Information Bulletin Number 487) (Feb. 1985).

4.   *See* R. Wasserstrom and R. Wiles, *Field Duty: U.S. Farmworkers and Pesticide Safety* 3 (World Resources Institute) (July 1985).

5.   EPA originally cancelled all uses of dinoseb, concluding that the chemical poses an "imminent hazard" to human health, but later modified its decision after industry appeals. Restrictions include prohibiting women of child-bearing age from contact with the chemical, requiring protective clothing, limiting sale of the chemical, and banning application in moderate or heavy winds. 51 Fed. Reg. 36634 (Oct. 14, 1986); U.S. Environmental Protection Agency, *Decision and Final Order Modifying Final Suspension of Pesticide Products Which Contain Dinoseb* (Office of Administrator) (Mar. 30, 1987); "Banning a Weedkiller: No Middle Ground," *The Washington Post* A1 (Aug. 3, 1987). In addition to risks to workers, dinoseb has been detected in the ground water of at least one state, New York. G. Hallberg, "From Hoes to Herbicides," 41 *Journal of Soil and Water Conservation* 360 (Nov.-Dec. 1986).

6.   W. Campbell, "Second Pesticide Study Indicates Cancer Link," *The Hartford Courant* A5 (Aug. 10, 1988).

7.   *See* "From Hoes to Herbicides," *supra* note 5, at 357-364; E. Nielsen and L. Lee, *The Magnitude and Costs of Groundwater Contamination from Agricultural Chemicals* (USDA-ERS Agricultural Economic Report No. 567) (June 1987).

8.   USDA, *The Second RCA Appraisal: Review Draft* 10-20, 10-21 (July 1987).

9.   *Id.*

10. *See* M. Fleming, "Agricultural Chemicals in Groundwater: Preventing Contamination by Removing Barriers Against Low-Input Farm Management," 2 *American Journal of Alternative Agriculture* 124 (Summer 1987).

11. *The Magnitude and Costs of Groundwater Contamination from Agricultural Chemicals, supra* note 7, at 19.

12. *Id.* at 1.

13. *Id.* at 20.

14. *Id.* at 5.

15. U.S. EPA, Alachlor; Notice of Intent to Cancel Registrations; Conclusion of Special Review, 52 Fed. Reg. 49,483 (Dec. 31, 1987).

16. U.S. EPA, *Aldicarb: Special Review Technical Support Document* 1 (Office of Pesticides and Toxic Substances) (June 1988).

17. G. Hallberg, "Agricultural Chemicals in Groundwater: Extent and Implications," 2 *American Journal of Alternative Agriculture* 8 (Winter 1987).

18. *Id.*

19. *See* S. Chapman and L. Carter, *Crop Production: Principles and Practices* 144 (1976). ("With irrigation, the fertilizer requirements of a crop may increase 50 percent or more.")

20. D. Armstrong and R. Strube, "Irrigation in Mason County, Ill: Implications for the Corn Belt," 22 *Crops and Soils* 13 (Nov. 1969).

21. "From Hoes to Herbicides," *supra* note 5 at 358.

22. J. AuCoin, *Water in Nebraska: Use, Politics, Policies* 11 (1984).

23. *Id.*

24. *The Magnitude and Costs of Groundwater Contamination from Agricultural Chemicals, supra* note 7, at 35.

25. *Id.* at 28.

26. USDA, *Economic Indicators of the Farm Sector: Costs of Production, 1985* 34 (USDA-ERS ECIFS 5-1) (Aug. 1986).

27. *Id.* at 84.

28.   *Handbook of Pest Management in Agriculture, Volume I* 3, 106 (D. Pimental, Ed.) (1981).

29.   *Id.*

30.   National Research Council, *Pesticide Resistance: Strategies and Tactics for Management* ix (Board on Agriculture) (1986).

31.   *Introduction to Insect Pest Management* 228 (R. Metcalf and W. Luckmann, Eds.) (1982).

32.   *Id.*

33.   *See generally* USDA, *Report and Recommendations on Organic Farming* (July 1980); *Introduction to Insect Pest Management, supra* note 31; *Proceedings of the Fifth International Symposium on Biological Control of Weeds* (E. Del Fosse, Ed.) (CSIRO, 1981); P. De Bach, *Biological Control By Natural Enemies* (1974).

34.   *Introduction to Insect Pest Management, supra* note 31, at 14-19.

35.   *See* D. Granatstein, *Reshaping the Bottom Line: On-Farm Strategies for a Sustainable Agriculture* 9-15 (Land Stewardship Project) (1988).

36.   *Introduction to Insect Management, supra* note 31, at 9-10, 504-505; *Technology, Public Policy, and the Changing Structure of American Agriculture, supra* note 1, at 58-59.

37.   W. Sinclair, "Organic Farming is Blossoming," *The Washington Post* A3 (Nov. 23, 1987).

38.   *Technology, Public Policy, and the Changing Structure of American Agriculture, supra* note 1, at 61, 62.

39.   *Pest Management Strategies in Crop Protection, Volume I, supra* note 2, at 6.

40.   *Economic Indicators of the Farm Sector: Costs of Production, 1985, supra* note 26, at 34.

41.   *Id.*

42.   National Center for Appropriate Technology, "ATTRA - Appropriate Technology Transfer for Rural Areas: A USDA Extension Program on Low-Input Farm and Community Resource Management," 3 (Mar. 23, 1987) (pamphlet).

43.   *Report and Recommendations on Organic Farming, supra* note 33, at 48.

44.   S. Postel, *Defusing the Toxics Threat: Controlling Pesticides and Industrial Waste* 29 (Worldwatch Institute Paper No. 79) (Sept. 1987).

45.   *Id.* at 30.

46.   *See, e.g., Report and Recommendations on Organic Farming, supra* note 33, at 16.

47.   *Technology, Public Policy, and the Changing Structure of American Agriculture, supra* note 1, at 61.

48.   Consulting firm of McMahon and Associates, "Low Input Agricultural Research," (June 1, 1987) (pamphlet).

49.   *Id.* at 6.

50.   *Id.* at 13.

51.   "IFM Completes Second Year With Projects in Most Counties," 2 *Integrated Farm Management Notes* 1 (Nov. 1988).

52.   "Stewardship Farmers Share On-Farm Research," 6 *The Land Stewardship Letter* 1 (Summer 1988).

53.   *Technology, Public Policy, and the Changing Structure of American Agriculture, supra* note 1, at 267; Joint Council on Food and Agricultural Sciences, *Five-Year Plan for the Food and Agricultural Sciences* 92 (USDA-Cooperative Extension Service) (Mar. 1986).

54.   *Five-Year Plan for the Food and Agricultural Sciences, supra* note 53, at 92.

55.   *Id.* at 261.

56.   M. Dover and L. Talbot, *To Feed the Earth: Agro-Ecology for Sustainable Development* 54 (World Resources Institute) (June 1987).

57.   *See, e.g.,* K. McNamara, "Research For Farmers, By Farmers," 9 *The New Farm* 18-22 (Sept.-Oct. 1987).

58.   Food Security Act of 1985, Pub. L. No. 99-198, Title XIV, Subtitle C, 99 Stat. 1354, 1461-1471, 7 U.S.C. §4701 - 4710.

59.   *See, e.g.,* "Soil and Water Conservation Concerns and Issues," Hearings before the Subcommittee on Conservation, Credit, and Rural Development of the House Committee on Agriculture, 98th Cong. 1st Sess. 422-423, 433-434 (May 4, 1983).

60.   Food Security Act of 1985, *supra* note 58, §1409, 99 Stat. 1546, 1547, 7 U.S.C. 450i(b).

61.   National Center for Appropriate Technology, *supra* note 42.

62.   *See* J. Harsch, "Who is LISA?" 1 *Organic Food Matters* 20-21 (1989).

63.   P. Madden *et al.*, "Low-Input/Sustainable Agriculture Research and Education Projects for 1988," (USDA Cooperative State Research Service) (1988).

64.   W. Sinclair, "Organic Farming Study Irks Fertilizer Industry," *The Washington Post* A3 (Mar. 17, 1988).

65.   National Center for Appropriate Technology, *supra* note 42, at 1.

66.   *Five-Year Plan for the Food and Agricultural Sciences, supra* note 53, at 92.

67.   USDA initially opposed the Agricultural Productivity Act, claiming that Department programs were adequately addressing the need for low-input agriculture research and extension. *See* Testimony of Dr. Clare I. Harris, Acting Administrator of the Cooperative State Research Service, U.S. Department of Agriculture, Hearings on the APA before the Subcommittee on Conservation, Credit and Rural Development of the House Agriculture Committee, 98th Cong., 1st Sess. 322-324 (Sept. 20, 1983). The Department later withdrew its objection.

68.   Such research is a critical-and often missing-component of agricultural research and extension. *See* D. Holt, "A Competitive R&D Strategy for U.S. Agriculture," 237 *Science* 1401-1402 (Sept. 18, 1987).

69.   *Pesticide Industry Sales and Usage: 1985 Market Estimates, supra* note 2, Table 2; USDA, *Agricultural Statistics 1986* 414 (Statistical Reporting Service) (1986).

70.   Farmers applied an average of 2.6 pounds or 42 ounces per acre of pesticides to field crops in 1980. A one percent reduction would lower per-acre applications by 0.42 ounce. W. Ferguson, *Pesticide Use on Selected Crops* 6 (USDA-ERS Ag. Info. Bull. No. 494) (June 1985).

71.   These excise taxes, imposed on the manufacture or sale of certain items, do not include "penalty" taxes. *See* Joint Committee on Taxation, "Schedule of Present Federal Excise Taxes (As of Apr. 1, 1987)," (JCS-13-87) (May 28, 1987).

72.   I.R.C. §9503.

73.   U.S. Office of Management and Budget, *Special Analyses: Budget of the United States Government*, FY 1988 C-15 (1987).

74.   I.R.C. §9502.

75.   *Special Analyses: Budget of the United States Government, FY 1988, supra* note 73, at C-16.

76.   U.S. Department of the Treasury, Internal Revenue Service, *Excise Taxes for 1987* 7-11 (Publication 510) (Oct. 1986).

77.   *See* Postel, *supra* note 44, at 48; M. Dover, *A Better Mousetrap: Improving Pest Management for Agriculture* 59 (World Resources Institute, Washington, D.C.) (Sept. 1985).

78.   *Des Moines Register*, "State Survey Confirms Fear of Polluted Water," A1 (Nov. 16, 1986).

79.   House Democratic Caucus, "The Iowa Groundwater Protection Act (HF 631)," 1-3 (June 16, 1987).

80.   *Id.* at 1.

81.   P. Holden, *Pesticides and Groundwater Quality: Issues and Problems in Farm States* 73 (Board on Agriculture, National Research Council) (1986).

5

The Rural Landscape–Proposals
for Farmland Taxation

Farmland is among the nation's most valuable natural assets. This chapter discusses how state differential tax provisions and various federal policies determine the fate of those farmlands most worth protecting and how those provisions and policies should be improved.

The Importance of Prime Farmland

Not all farmland is created equal. Some of the most productive is defined in federal laws and regulations as "prime" farmland, or that with "the best combination of physical and chemical characteristics" for raising agricultural products with "minimum inputs of fuel, fertilizer, pesticides, and labor, and without intolerable soil erosion."[1] This is echoed more succinctly in a USDA appraisal of soil and water conditions that describes prime farmland as "land on which crops can be produced for the least cost and with the least damage to the resource base."[2] Among the most important factors in determining whether land meets these standards are climatic conditions, the prevalence of rocks, and soil salinity, moisture, drainage, erodibility, acidity and susceptibility to flooding.

According to USDA estimates, this nation has some 342 million acres of prime farmland, an area roughly equivalent to 18 percent of the continental United States.[3] Most of this land is devoted to the production of rowcrops, livestock or timber. Each of the 50 states contains some prime farmland, with the largest concentrations in the nation's heartland. More than one-third is located in the Corn Belt and the Northern Plains regions.[4]

Not all farmland worth protecting meets the traditional definition of prime farmland, however. In some cases, fields with apparently inferior natural attributes outperform "prime" farmland in terms of crop yields and farm income.[5]

To an extent, applicable federal policy recognizes the need to protect some nonprime land. In particular, laws and regulations governing the Soil Conservation Service recognize the importance of "unique" farmland used for production of high-value crops such as fruits and vegetables.[6] The federal statutes and rules also afford special status to farmland not technically prime or unique but nevertheless identified by state or local jurisdictions as important.[7] The principal methodology developed by SCS for predicting the likely consequences of farmland conversion—the "Land Evaluation and Site Assessment" system—accounts not just for the intrinsic capability of land for farm production, but also for various social and geographic factors that determine the value of particular places for agriculture.[8]

The steady march of asphalt and concrete poses serious threats to all of these categories of important farmland. During the 24-year span from 1958 to 1982, an estimated 30 million acres of farmland were converted to urban uses.[9] Today's conversion rates have moderated from those of the 1970s development boom, but approximately one million agricultural acres continue to give way to built-up sprawl each year.[10] The problem is most serious at the ever-widening metropolitan fringe, which bears a close spatial correspondence to those of the nation's counties where farming makes the greatest economic contribution.[11]

In some regions, the decline in farmland acreage and the number of farms has been precipitous. Noting that his state depends on outside sources for 85 percent of its food, a former Massachusetts Agriculture Commissioner recently expressed concern over the shrinkage of the Commonwealth's farmland base from more than two million acres in 1945 to less than 700,000 acres in 1981.[12] From 1959 to 1982, cropland in the Northeast region as a whole was reduced 19 percent, principally as a consequence of urban expansion.[13]

Significant as they are, these findings understate the impact of urban growth on agriculture. USDA economists have pointed out that "even the prospect" of development "can undermine

In 1980, the landscape of downtown Richmond, Virginia, provided a striking contrast to farming operations in Henrico County. *Photo by Jim McCabe; courtesy of USDA Soil Conservation Service.*

the longrun productivity of agricultural lands and cause greater idling of agricultural land than would otherwise be the case."[14] Although difficult to quantify precisely, there are indications of an "impermanence syndrome" whereby farmers anticipating a financial windfall from selling land to developers withhold traditional investments in agricultural buildings, machinery, and soil and water conservation.[15] Moreover, metropolitan growth often fragments "critical land masses," areas of sufficient size and contiguity to sustain economically productive farming units.[16]

Some government officials have argued that these trends present no cause for concern. Former Assistant Secretary of Agriculture John B. Crowell stated in 1984 that "it's greatly premature to be concerned by–or to be doing anything about–a possible shortage of good cropland."[17] In a 1987 appraisal of agricultural resource conditions, USDA concluded optimistically that technological progress over the next several decades will boost productivity sufficiently to compensate for prime farmland loss and other environmental problems in meeting demand for farm products.[18]

Such complacency could be dangerously shortsighted. The history of natural resource management in this country testifies amply to the capriciousness of supply and demand forecasts. In addition, the model scenarios underlying USDA's optimistic appraisal were constructed without regard to weather and climate, factors the document candidly identifies as "an extremely important set of conditions."[19] Among the omitted considerations are the prospective agricultural impacts of global warming induced by atmospheric greenhouse effect, a matter of growing scientific concern.[20]

Moreover, the loss of good farmland may bring environmental harms that stand apart from any issue of long-term food security. In particular, the burden of meeting future demand may shift to more marginal fields with severe nutrient limitations and inferior moisture retention capability. As preceding chapters have suggested, farmers already tend to overcompensate for such conditions with massive applications of synthetic chemical fertilizers and installation of new irrigation facilities. This exacerbates water pollution problems, raises production costs and, potentially, causes consumer prices to escalate.[21]

The march of suburbia has encroached on American agriculture, as illustrated by this prime farmland near Chicago, Illinois, advertised for sale in 1983. *Photo by Jim McCabe; courtesy of USDA Soil Conservation Service.*

In addition, the rural landscape itself is an environmental amenity worth saving. Recognizing the aesthetic importance of agriculture in urban design, noted metropolitan planner Ian McHarg has observed that "the farm is the basic factory–the farmer is the country's best landscape gardener and maintenance work force, the custodian of much scenic beauty."[22] Similarly, Ralph Grossi, President of the American Farmland Trust, argues that losing farmland means "[n]ot only ... that we must bring our food from farther away–along with higher prices and lower quality–but ... the loss of the green spaces that grace our surroundings and of a heritage that is as old as our country itself."[23]

Echoing these sentiments, agricultural experiment station researchers in the Northeast have observed:

> First, the maintenance of a local agricultural sector broadens local economic diversity and strengthens local multiplier effects. Second, farmland generates significant nonmarket benefits, such as watershed maintenance and wildlife habitat. Third, there is a social risk cost to development, since development generally is irreversible while preservation is not. Fourth, a local farmland resource allows the nearby population to limit its dependence on imported food and the more complicated national and international food distribution infrastructures. Farmland provides rural pastoral scenes, recreational opportunities, and direct market access to food (including pick-your-own opportunities). It is also tangible proof of the nation's agrarian heritage. There are general social concerns that happen to support the objectives of farm people to remain economically viable in their chosen profession.[24]

Ranging from the aesthetic to the purely pragmatic, these reasons form a compelling case for conservation.

State Tax Laws and Their Shortcomings

Maintenance of a thriving agriculture industry is a common policy objective for the states. Executive orders issued by the governors of Illinois and several other midwestern states affirm the importance of farmland retention and, in some cases, direct state agencies to avoid contributing to excessive farmland loss.[25]

Among the wide variety of conservation strategies, tax relief is the most common and in some cases the only way state governments seek to keep farmland in farming. Most evidence suggests, however, that the breaks on state taxes enable certain rural landowners to reap sizable savings but do little to ensure long-term retention of good farmland in agriculture. Several improvements could be tailored to remedy inadequacies in existing laws.

Since Maryland led the way in 1956,[26] nearly every state has adopted a differential or "use value" mechanism that assesses farmland according to its value for agriculture rather than its potentially higher value for development.[27] Two states, Wisconsin and Michigan, award income tax credits in lieu of adjustments in valuation; these may be claimed by farmers if their property tax liabilities exceed a specified percentage of their incomes.[28]

In its simplest form, use value assessment confers tax savings unconditionally. This is the case in 19 states, including those covering much of the Corn Belt and the Great Plains (Figure 2).[29]

A majority of states, however, allow only for deferral of taxes, requiring payment if the land is converted to non-agricultural uses. The most common of these "recapture" devices is the rollback penalty, under which a taxpayer who sells farmland to a developer must refund any differential tax saving—sometimes with interest—that was realized while the affected property was retained in farming.[30] An alternative used by several states, including Connecticut and Vermont, is a transfer tax imposed as a percentage of profits from sales involving removal of land from agriculture.[31]

A few states require landowners to agree to multi-year restrictive covenants in order to benefit from preferential agricultural use taxation. In Pennsylvania, taxpayers must agree to keep their farmland in agriculture for at least 10 years to qualify; the covenant term is automatically extended by one year annually unless the landowner serves notice that he does not wish to renew.[32]

Use value assessment has proven to be a politically palatable technique, for the most part avoiding the controversy that often surrounds debates over public appropriations or land use regulation.[33] It has encountered legal complications, however. In particular, some courts have found the programs contrary to the clauses of state constitutions requiring uniform taxation of real estate.[34]

Figure 2

State Differential Tax Assessment Laws

☐ Preferential tax assessment only

☐ Preferential tax assessment with deferred taxation

▨ Preferential tax assessment with land transfer taxes

▨ Preferential tax assessment with restrictive agreements
and penalties for withdrawal

Sources: K. Grillo and D. Seld, *State Laws Relating to Preferential Assessment of Farmland* 4 (USDA-ERS, Natural Resource Economics Division) (June 1987); S.B. Klein, *Agricultural Land Preservation: A Review of State Programs and Their Natural Resource Data Requirements* 9 (National Conference of State Legislatures) (Jan. 1982); University of Vermont Agricultural Experiment Station, "Use Value Assessment of Agricultural Land in the Northeast," 13 (Bulletin 694) (May 1987).

This was the initial fate of Maryland's seminal use value assessment law.[35] A number of states, including Maryland, have now amended their constitutions explicitly to permit the taxation of some land at less than its full market value.[36]

Use value assessment can be highly lucrative for rural landowners. The tax savings tend to be greatest at the metropolitan fringe, where some farmland owners pay as little as five percent of what their tax liability would be under a highest value formulation.[37] Collectively, nearly three-quarters of a billion dollars in property value was exempted from taxation in 1985 under New York's agricultural value assessment program.[38]

While use value assessment is primarily intended to insulate farmers wishing to remain in agriculture from financial pressure to sell their property to developers, it also helps promote equivalence between the amount of property tax paid and the level of public services received. In this context, Virginia's Piedmont Environmental Council has noted that "even when taxed at use value, rural lands generate far more tax dollars than they require in service dollars."[39] A recent American Farmland Trust study found that for every $1.00 in collected taxes, just $0.11 was required for public services on farmland and open space, whereas $1.28 was required to serve sprawling low-density residential development.[40] Clearly, "[A] disproportionately large property tax burden on farmland cannot be supported on the basis of taxation in relation to benefits received."[41]

Nevertheless, differential property taxation often does not guarantee long-term retention of prime farmland. For example, the Michigan tax credit program has attracted robust enrollment of farmland in parts of the state with minor development pressures, but very little enrollment close to urban areas.[42]

In general, the tax savings for maintaining agricultural uses are insufficient to outbid sale prices offered by developers.[43] As a result, farmland owners often can simply take advantage of sizable tax savings while speculatively waiting for land values to appreciate.[44] Where rollback requirements or transfer taxes are in effect, the farmland owner may simply enjoy the equivalent of a low-interest or interest-free loan while holding property for later conversion.

Even the restrictive covenants imposed by some states as a condition of tax benefits do not necessarily ensure long-term farmland retention. As planning expert Peter Wolf asserts in *Land in America*, "[T]he farmer or the speculator can wait for the period of agreement to expire and then sell. Stated bluntly, there is nothing in any of these [state differential taxation laws] that assures the continuation of prime farmland in its agricultural use. Each is a palliative to buy time, literally, through the use of an indirect subsidy."[45]

Wolf observes further that most state tax programs fail to differentiate properly among various types of rural land. He notes that "[v]ast stretches of marginal cropland, pasture, and timberlands of all sorts are included in the same legislation calculated to promote preservation of prime agricultural land."[46] A related shortcoming is that most state tax laws award use value benefits without regard to stewardship practices. In most cases, someone who abusively plows a wetland or a field susceptible to excessive soil erosion is just as likely to receive preferential tax treatment as someone who conserves soil and water in producing crops on high quality farmland.

Recommendations for Improving State Laws

Three principles should guide improvement of these state laws. First, and most generally, the states should not use differential taxation in a vacuum, as a surrogate for multi-dimensional farmland programs. A related conclusion was drawn by the 1981 National Agricultural Lands Study. This report urged that, despite its shortcomings, differential taxation is a "valuable component" when used in a "comprehensive agricultural land protection program."[47] Put another way, preferential tax policy should be an adjunct to, not the centerpiece of, the states' efforts to conserve farmland.

Some state laws provide useful models for linking preferential taxation to complementary programs. In particular, by one count taken in 1987, there are 14 programs for purchase of development rights in various parts of the country, under which state or local governments pay landowners the difference between the affected property's market value and its agricultural use value.[48] This compensation is awarded in exchange for long-term restrictive covenants barring urban conversion.*

---

* Massachusetts has reported particularly strong success with its Agricultural Preservation Restriction program. From 1978 through 1986, the program
(continued...)

Preferential taxation can also complement state planning laws such as those in California and Oregon that seek to preserve agricultural land use within comprehensive growth management programs.[49] In a related context, state tax laws can sometimes be structured to provide incentive for local governments to initiate farmland protection programs. In Wisconsin, differential income tax credits are restricted to residents of counties where agricultural land policies meet certain protective specifications.[50] In Maryland, revenue from land transfer taxes is placed into a state-administered fund for conservation purposes such as purchase of farmland development rights.[51] This approach derives from the sensible notion that public revenue originating from the depletion of a nonrenewable resource should be used to secure a conservation legacy for future generations.*

Some states have even coupled their farmland protection programs with other social objectives. In Vermont, for example, the state legislature recently appropriated $3 million for development projects serving both low-income housing needs and retention of rural open space and historic properties.[52]

Second, all states should require that beneficiaries of use value assessment abide by protective covenants with rollback penalties or land transfer taxes to recapture lost revenue in the event of departures from the agreements. The penalties should be made stiff enough to discourage nonagricultural land conversion and to ensure that states recoup fully their investments in farmland protection. To help achieve this end, interest at market rates should be assessed on all rollback payments.

Higher penalties would entail some risk that farmland owners might be deterred from entering state conservation programs. As agricultural experiment station researchers in the Northeast

---

*(...continued)
obtained deed restrictions on more than 16,000 acres prohibiting all uses that ruin the lands' farming capabilities. By the end of 1987, the figure had risen to nearly 20,000 protected farmland acres.

* Some have argued that such taxes also should be imposed at the federal level. For example, legislation (S.1338) introduced in 1987 by Senator Chafee (R-RI) would have imposed transfer taxes on large-scale real estate transactions to fund a national trust for open space acquisition.

theorize, "[S]tates apparently assume that when penalties for withdrawal are sufficiently high to discourage use change, the number of landowners who enter the program will be small."[53] Nevertheless, the risks appear reasonable. The same researchers observe that "[n]o state has tried effective penalty levels to test this assumption," and they urge increased penalties as a "reasonable response" to the ineffective *status quo*.[54]

Third, land stewardship conditions should accompany property tax benefits or income tax credits calculated through use value assessment. In particular, the benefits should not reward farming practices that cause excessive soil erosion, water depletion or wetlands destruction. In this regard, more states should borrow a chapter from the Wisconsin program and require that beneficiaries implement approved conservation plans.[55]

Federal Law and Policy

The prospects for success of the states' preferential tax programs would also be enhanced substantially by a strong federal commitment to conserving prime and other important farmland. Most important, this must include uncompromising support for the Farmland Protection Policy Act (FPPA). Enacted in 1981, the law identifies certain categories of farmland as constituting "a unique natural resource" that must be conserved,[56] and seeks "to minimize the extent to which Federal programs contribute to the unnecessary and irreversible conversion of farmland to nonagricultural uses."[57]

Enactment of the FPPA was Congress' response to a finding of the National Agricultural Lands Study that federal activities contribute significantly to farmland loss across the country.[58] Federally-sponsored highways, airports, wastewater treatment plants and housing developments are important examples.[59] The statute requires federal agencies to assess the impacts of proposed activities on farmland and evaluate the feasibility of alternatives that would avoid or minimize potential conversion.[60] Under the Act, each "department, agency, independent commission or other unit of the federal government" must conform its policies and programs to this mandate.[61]

The FPPA's other leading purpose is "to assure that Federal programs are administered in a manner that, to the extent practicable, will be compatible with State ... local government, and private programs and policies to protect farmland." This provision was reinforced in 1985 by strengthening amendments that allow states to seek judicial relief in situations where federal actions run roughshod on the state programs.[62]

The FPPA's emphasis on intergovernmental consistency has special relevance for preferential taxation, the most ubiquitous state prescription for farmland protection. When the federal government is the agent of nonagricultural conversion, states' attempts to reward protection through reduced property taxes can be frustrated.

Unfortunately, implementation of the FPPA has been weak. USDA delayed a key rulemaking for more than three years following the law's enactment in 1981.[63] The final rule, issued in 1984, rendered the law virtually toothless by prohibiting federal agencies from withholding assistance for conversion projects, even if reviews identify unavoidable adverse consequences.[64] In general, the federal government has done very little to enforce the law's purposes.

A shift in thinking is sorely needed. A first step toward curing the problem should be promulgation of a new farmland protection rule proposed by USDA in January 1987.[65] That rule would implement the strengthening amendments enacted in 1985 and, among other things, reverse the prohibition on denial of federal assistance when developers have not bothered to conduct a proper search for alternatives to converting good farmland.

Proper implementation of the FPPA should also bring a systematic review of how the federal government influences the fate of this nation's farmland. The law specifies that every unit of the U.S. government:

> shall review current provisions of law, administrative rules and regulations, and policies and procedures applicable to it to determine whether any provision thereof will prevent such unit of the Federal government from taking appropriate action to comply fully with the provisions of [the FPPA ... and], as appropriate, develop proposals for action to bring its programs, authorities, and administrative activities into conformity with the purpose and policy of [the FPPA].[66]

With respect to taxation, the Department of the Treasury and its Internal Revenue Service should conduct a thorough inventory of the federal tax code, identifying features that create a bias for nonagricultural prime farmland conversion. The task should result in recommendations for changes in statutory authority needed to align federal tax policy with the purposes of the Act.

While an exhaustive study is beyond the scope of this work, among the remaining tax preferences that warrant a close look in such a review are the following:

• *Tax-exempt bonds.* The Revenue Code exempts from taxation interest income derived from industrial development bonds. These bonds are sold to taxpayers by state or local governments to finance development that in many cases consumes vast areas of farmland. For example, development bonds are a popular means of financing certain multi-family rental housing projects, airports, docks and wharves, mass transit projects, waste disposal sites and facilities to provide local energy and water supplies.[67]

• *Real estate development deductions.* Owners of rental dwellings or any nonresidential real estate benefit from accelerated depreciation as well as mortgage interest deductions. For owner-occupied residences and vacation homes, mortgage interest expenses and property taxes are deductible. These important tax subsidies create a bias for built development on farmland.

• *Tax credits for rental housing.* The 1986 Tax Reform Act created a generous new tax credit for development of rental dwellings for low-income tenants.[68] Basically, the credit is worth up to nine percent of investments in construction or rehabilitation of low-income rental units[69] and can be claimed annually for ten years. An additional annual credit of up to four percent is available to offset the costs of acquiring existing low-income housing structures.[70]*

---

* The Vermont program described earlier in this chapter provides encouraging evidence that the laudable goal of providing ample housing for low-income persons need not conflict with protecting the nation's best farmland from non-agricultural conversion. The Vermont bill was modeled after a successful private land trust program for rehabilitating historic buildings for the elderly.

After an appropriate review, Congress should amend the tax code to withhold subsidies found to assist unnecessary and harmful farmland conversion.

Chapter Notes

1.   Farmland Protection Policy Act §1540(c)(1)(A), 7 U.S.C. §4201(c)(1)(A) [hereinafter FPPA]. *See also* 7 C.F.R. §657.5(a).

2.   USDA, *The Second RCA Appraisal: Review Draft* 3-12 (July-Aug. 1987).

3.   USDA Soil Conservation Service, *1982 National Resources Inventory, Basic Statistics* Table 40(a) (Statistical Bulletin No. 756) (Sept. 1987).

4.   *Id.*

5.   *See, e.g.,* N. Bills *et al.,* "Crop Yields and Net Income on Prime Farmland in New York," (A.E. Res. 84-21, Dept. of Ag. Economics, Cornell Univ., Ithica, NY) (1984).

6.   7 C.F.R. §657.5(b). To qualify as "unique," farmland must possess site characteristics such as soils, moisture, slope and nearness to market favorable to production of a specific high value crop.

7.   *Id.* §657.5(c) and (d).

8.   *See* F. Steiner, "Agricultural Land Evaluation and Site Assessment in the United States: An Introduction," 11 *Environmental Management* 375-377 (1987).

9.   *The Second RCA Appraisal: Review Draft, supra* note 2, at 3-8.

10. *Id.* at 3-9.

11. American Farmland Trust, "Farming on the Fringe" (map) (1986). This source defines "high market value farming counties" as "those top 20 percent of counties in each state which produced the highest market value of farm products in at least two out of three Agricultural Census years: 1974, 1978, and 1982."

12. F. Winthrop, Jr., "Saving Farms, Massachusetts Style," *Blair and Ketchum's Country Journal* (Dec. 1981).

13. University of Vermont Agricultural Experiment Station, "Use Value Assessment of Agricultural Land in the Northeast," 5 (Bulletin 694) (May 1987). In this study, the northeastern region comprises Connecticut, Delaware, Maine, Maryland, Massachusetts, New Hampshire, New Jersey, New York, Pennsylvania, Rhode Island, Vermont and West Virginia. *See also* J. Mackenzie and G. Cole,

"Use-Value Assessment as a Farmland Preservation Policy" in *Sustaining Agriculture Near Cities* 251 (William Lockertz, Ed.) (1988).

14. G. Gustafson and N. Bills, *U.S. Cropland, Urbanization, and Landowner-ship Patterns* 1 (USDA-ERS, Agricultural Economic Report No. 520) (Nov. 1984).

15. R. Dunford, "The Development and Current Status of Federal Farmland Retention Policy," 74-75 (CRS Report No. 85-21 ENR) (Nov. 21, 1984).

16. "Use Value Assessment ... in the Northeast," *supra* note 13, at ii.

17. John B. Crowell, Jr., Assistant Secretary of Agriculture for Natural Resources and Environment, Speech to the Private Lands and Water Committee, National Cattlemen's Association, New Orleans, Jan. 24, 1984.

18. *See The Second RCA Appraisal: Review Draft, supra* note 2, at 12-2, 12-14.

19. *Id.* at 12-6.

20. *See, e.g.,* D. Abrahamson and P. Ciborowski, "Harvest of Sand: Agriculture's Future in a Changing Climate," 5 *The Amicus Journal* 38-44 (Spring 1984).

21. *See* Dunford, *supra* note 15, at 72-73.

22. I. McHarg, *Design With Nature* 60 (1971).

23. R. Grossi, "Farmland v. Shopping Centers," *The Washington Post* A26 (Nov. 19, 1988).

24. "Use Value Assessment ... in the Northeast," *supra* note 13, at 4.

25. H. Hiemstra and N. Bushwick, "How States are Saving Farmland," 6 *American Land Forum Magazine* 63 (Spring 1986).

26. USDA/Council on Environmental Quality, National Agricultural Lands Study, *An Inventory of State and Local Programs to Protect Farmland* 1 (Sept. 1981).

27. *See* NASDA Research Foundation Farmland Project, "Current State Farmland Protection Activities" (Table) (Jan. 1987).

28. Hiemstra and Bushwick, *supra* note 25, at 62. Approximately 11 million acres of land have been enrolled in these states' tax credit programs.

29.   K. Grillo and D. Seid, *State Laws Relating to Preferential Assessment of Farmland* 3 (USDA-ERS Staff Report No. AGES870326) (June 1987).

30.   *Id.*

31.   S. Klein, *Agricultural Land Preservation: A Review of State Programs and their Natural Resource Data Requirements* 9 (National Conference of State Legislatures) (Jan. 1982).

32.   E. Roberts, *The Law and the Preservation of Agricultural Land* 48 (1982).

33.   C. Hickman, "Preserving Rural Lands," 85 *Journal of Forestry* 33 (Mar. 1987).

34.   USDA/Council on Environmental Quality, National Agricultural Lands Study, *The Protection of Farmland: A Reference Guidebook for State and Local Governments* 268-270 (1981) [hereinafter NALS Reference Guidebook].

35.   Roberts, *supra* note 32, at 46.

36.   NALS Reference Guidebook, *supra* note 34, at 30.

37.   L. Borie, "Use Value Assessment: Tax Break or Management Incentive?" 93 *American Forests* 47 (May/June 1987).

38.   State of New York, Board of Equalization and Assessment, "Agricultural Value Assessment Impact Update," 12-14 (July 1987).

39.   "Use Value Tax Discussions Begin," *Piedmont Environmental Council Newsreporter* 2 (Warrenton, VA) (May 1987).

40.   American Farmland Trust, *Density-Related Public Costs* 41A (1986).

41.   "Use Value Assessment ... in the Northeast," *supra* note 13, at 2.

42.   S. Hoffmann, "Farmland and Open Space Preservation in Michigan: An Empirical Analysis," 19 *Journal of Law Reform* 1162 (Summer 1986).

43.   Hickman, *supra* note 33, at 33.

44.   Borie, *supra* note 37, at 47.

45.   P. Wolf, *Land in America: Its Value, Use and Control* 510 (1981).

46.   *Id.*

47.   U.S. Department of Agriculture/Council on Environmental Quality, *National Agricultural Lands Study: Final Report* 69 (Jan. 1981) [hereinafter NALS Final Report].

48.   J. Buckland, "The History and Use of Purchase of Development Rights in the United States," 14 *Landscape and Urban Planning* 246-247 (1987). The jurisdictions with PDR programs, listed chronologically, include Suffolk County, New York; Burlington County, New Jersey; Maryland; Massachusetts; Connecticut; Howard County, Maryland; King County, Washington; New Hampshire; Easthampton Township, New York; Southhampton Township, New York; New Jersey; Rhode Island; Hunterdon County, New Jersey; and Forsyth County, North Carolina.

49.   *See* M. Duncan, "Agriculture as a Resource: Statewide Land Use Programs for the Preservation of Farmland," 14 *Ecology Law Quarterly* 401-483 (1987).

50.   NALS Reference Guidebook, *supra* note 34, at 214.

51.   Maryland Code, Article 81, §278 F(h).

52.   "Land Conservation Linked to Low-Income Housing in Vermont," *The New American Land* 4 (Sept./Oct. 1987).

53.   "Use Value Assessment ... in the Northeast," *supra* note 13, at 18.

54.   *Id.*

55.   Grillo and Seid, *supra* note 29, at 145.

56.   Within the FPPA, "farmland" comprises prime farmland, "unique" farmland important to production of high-value crops like fruits and vegetables, and other farmland "of statewide or local importance." FPPA §1540(c)(1), 7 U.S.C. §4201(c)(1).

57.   FPPA §1540(b), 7 U.S.C. §4201(b).

58.   NALS Final Report, *supra* note 47, at 48.

59.   *See* H. Hiemstra *et al.*, "Case Studies of Federal Activities," in *Agricultural Land Availability* 389 (Senate Agriculture Committee Print) (July 1981).

60.   FPPA §1541(b), 7 U.S.C. §4202(b).

61.   FPPA §1542(a), 7 U.S.C. §4203(a).

62.   The Food Security Act of 1985, Pub. L. No. 99-198, §1255(b), 99 Stat. 1354, 1518, 7 U.S.C. §4202.

63.   NRDC *et al.*, Comments on 7 C.F.R. §658 (Implementation of the Farmland Protection Policy Act) (1984).

64.   7 C.F.R. §658.3(c) (1984).

65.   USDA, Revision of Farmland Protection Policy Act, 52 Fed. Reg. 1465 (proposed Jan. 14, 1987).

66.   FPPA §§1542(a),(b), 7 U.S.C. §§4203(a),(b).

67.   H.R. Rep. No. 841, 99th Cong., 2d Sess. II-697 (Reporting of the Conference Committee to Accompany H.R. 3838, the Tax Reform Act of 1986) [hereinafter TRA Conference Report]. The TRA repealed previous authority for tax-exempt bond financing of facilities for sports, conventions or trade shows. *Id.* at II-700. Also of possible benefit to prime farmland protection, the TRA created special new authority for tax-exempt bond financing of redevelopment projects in blighted urban areas. *Id.* at II-718.

68.   Tax Reform Act of 1986, Pub. L. No. 99-514, §252, 100 Stat. 2085, 2189-2208. These credits replace other low-income housing benefits previously in the tax code. Various conditions govern receipt of the subsidy. For example, the law specifies a rather liberal minimum set-aside requirement that at least 20 percent of housing development projects must be occupied by low-income tenants. The Tax Reform Act also imposed a 15-year compliance period during which this condition must be satisfied, lest the Internal Revenue Service seek to recapture some of the awarded credits.

69.   I.R.C. §42. The situation is complicated by intricate formulae for computing the creditable portion of real estate investments, as well as the percentage of those shares that may actually be claimed on tax returns.

70.   *Id.*

6

Conservation Easements–New Applications for Sustainable Agriculture

An easement is a legal right, short of full ownership, to a specified use of real property. Easements are common in real estate law, routinely securing rights-of-way for sidewalks, utility lines, alleys and driveways. In most cases, easements operate to restrict the rights of the land owner so that the rights of the easement holder may be exercised freely.

Easements may be exchanged like other market goods and services. Some are of limited duration, while others apply in perpetuity to current and future owners of the affected property. Since easements by definition are held by someone other than the principal property owner, transactions involving the property do not affect an easement unless the easement holder consents to a modification.

This chapter examines easements in the context of agricultural conservation. The discussion examines circumstances in which tax law can aid the creation of beneficial easements and presents recommendations for additional policy incentives to strengthen this useful conservation tool.

Conservation Easements Generally

Easements have long been used in this country for land and natural resource protection. In appropriate circumstances, they can provide significant environmental protection at far less cost for both acquisition and administration than full ownership. For example, a simple form of conservation easement might transfer to a conservation organization the right to construct buildings on a parcel of open space, in effect prohibiting such construction without the organization's consent and, thus, protecting a scenic vista. Conservation easements typically are held and enforced either by private conservation organizations or agencies of government.

Some of the first long-term conservation easements were obtained by the National Park Service in the 1930s and 1940s to preserve scenic views along the Blue Ridge Parkway in North Carolina and Virginia and along the Natchez Trace Parkway in Mississippi, Alabama and Tennessee.[1] Programs administered by the U.S. Fish and Wildlife Service have placed more than one million acres of wetlands under permanent protective easement.[2]

More recently, conservation easements have been used by the private sector. For example, The Nature Conservancy, a national nonprofit organization, purchases and accepts donations of easements as part of its ambitious program to protect threatened plants, wildlife and ecosystems.[3] Another national organization, the American Farmland Trust, frequently uses easements to keep high-quality agricultural land in farming; the Trust was responsible for the first private farmland conservation easements in Michigan, Wisconsin and North Carolina.[4]

A wide variety of local private organizations have become widespread and important agents of easement acquisition. Perhaps the most important of these are local land trusts; as of 1985, 152 trusts in 34 states reported having conservation easement programs in place.[5]

The extensive private sector involvement in land conservation is welcome, given current constraints on public budgets. For example, the 1987 appropriation for the Land and Water Conservation Fund, the principal instrument for federal land acquisition, amounted to less than one-third the 1978 level.[6] Moreover, as one conservation writer has observed, "The 1980s are a time when few local governments can brag of revenue surpluses or strong voter support for large bond packages for acquiring parkland."[7]

There are many public advantages to conservation easements. While providing significant cost advantage over full ownership, properly constructed easements nevertheless "run with the land," remaining in force upon sale, inheritance or other transfer of the protected property. Less transitory than zoning ordinances and other forms of land use control, easements thus help guarantee a conservation legacy for future generations. Moreover, by retaining property in private ownership, easements often have only modest impacts on state and local tax revenue.

For private landowners, easement donation has become an increasingly common form of philanthropy. A recent survey of approximately 500 government and private conservation organizations found that one-fourth the land reported as protected under easement (more than 460,000 acres) had been donated.[8] Landowner concern for long-term environmental protection is the main motivating force in such donations; as the Maryland Environmental Trust has put it, "Most landowners who are interested in land conservation have ... a desire to see their property remain largely undeveloped–perhaps as a farm, woodland or natural area–even after their ownership comes to an end."[9]

Taxation of Conservation Easements

At present, tax benefits constitute the federal government's principal instrument for rewarding easement donors. Congress first enacted tax benefits for charitable gifts of "less than fee" interests in land in 1964.[10] The key Internal Revenue Code provision is section 170(h), which enables taxpayers to claim charitable contribution deductions for gifts of conservation easements.*

To qualify, easement restrictions must be enforceable in perpetuity and donated "exclusively for conservation purposes" to a "qualified organization."[11] "Conservation purposes" comprise four categories:

1) the preservation of land areas for outdoor recreation by, or the education of, the general public;

2) the protection of relatively natural habitat for fish, wildlife, or plants;

3) the preservation of open space (including farmland and forest land)... for the scenic enjoyment of the

---

* Section 170(h) departs from a general proscription against tax deductions for gifts of "partial interests" in real property.

general public, or in keeping with the twin test of a)
being pursuant to a clearly delineated Federal, State
or local governmental conservation policy and b)
providing significant public benefit; or

4) the preservation of an historically important land
area or certified historic structure.[12]

Of these, the open space category is the most important for
easements relating to agriculture. "Qualified organizations"
basically include units of government or tax-exempt private
entities such as land trusts.

After much delay, the Treasury Department published a final
rule implementing section 170(h) in January of 1986.[13] The
absence of a final rule for more than five years had created a
chilling effect on prospective easement donors who were
reluctant to proceed in the absence of certainty as to which
factual situations might qualify.

The final regulation interprets the open space category at
some length, setting explicit criteria as to what constitutes
"clearly delineated governmental policy" favoring preservation
and "significant public benefit." With respect to the first test,
the regulation states that "[a] general declaration of conservation
goals by a single official or legislative body is not sufficient" to
qualify as "clearly delineated."[14] Instead, the rule states that the
requirement will be met by donations that "further a specific,
identified conservation project" such as the preservation of a
wild and scenic river or a state program for flood prevention
and control.

The regulation lists 11 factors that may be considered in
determinations of "significant public benefit."[15] Notable examples
include "uniqueness of the property" within its geographic
setting, levels of built development in the vicinity and the
consistency between the easement and public conservation
programs. Cross referencing the "governmental policy" test, the
regulation provides that "[t]he more specific the governmental
policy with respect to the particular site to be protected, the
more likely the governmental decision, by itself, will tend to

establish the significant public benefit associated with the donation."[16]

Agricultural Applications

Most conservation easements are now designed to preserve existing natural scenery, special physiographic features, ecosystem integrity, pastoral landscapes or historic artifacts. Enormous untapped potential resides, however, in easements to adjust existing land uses for environmental protection. Among those urging wider application of easements for agricultural conservation is Duane Sand, Director of the Iowa Natural Heritage Foundation's Resourceful Farming Project.[17] Sand recommends that conservation easements, heretofore the province of "wildlife managers, land preservationists, water control officers and recreation planners," be used specifically to promote sustainable and environmentally sound farming practices.[18] Notable existing and promising applications include the following:

Farmland Protection. One of the most obvious applications is the preservation of farmland for farming. As noted, the Revenue Code makes special reference to farmland within the open space category, as does the regulation. However, as Stephen Small, a leading expert on conservation easements, has pointed out:

> This is not a farmland preservation statute; the inclusion of farmland and forestland in the statute means that an open space easement on farmland or forestland will be tested against the same standards (clearly delineated governmental policy, scenic enjoyment, and significant public benefit...) as will an easement on a vacant downtown lot, or on open land between the highway and the ocean, or on fifty undeveloped acres in the path of advancing urban sprawl.[19]

On the basis of the statutory language and selected IRS rulings, Small has concluded that "farmland for farmland's sake, without more, is not enough to qualify for a deductible conservation easement."[20]

Nevertheless, a significant amount of important farmland should qualify under the §170(h) criteria. In particular, the Treasury regulation cites two examples of government policy directly relevant to farmland. One is "the preservation of farmland pursuant to a state program for flood prevention and control;"* the other is "a government program according preferential tax assessment or preferential zoning for certain property deemed worthy of protection for conservation purposes."[21] The second example theoretically is broad indeed, as nearly every state offers preferential property tax assessment of farmland (Chapter 5).[22]

Once land passes the "governmental policy" test, it must then meet the "significant public benefit" test.[23] In practice, IRS has ruled favorably on donations of farmland easements where there has been significant development pressure in the affected area.[24]

Some farmland–particularly if near popular travel routes or tourist areas–may be able to bypass the government policy and public benefit tests altogether and qualify for open space easements by providing "for the scenic enjoyment of the general public."[25] In making determinations on this ground, the IRS weighs such factors as "compatibility of the land use with other land in the vicinity," "degree of contrast and variety provided by the visual scene" and "harmonious variety of shapes and textures."[26]

As noted, all tax-deductible conservation easements must be made "exclusively for conservation purposes."[27] This can disqualify an easement that serves one of the four specified conservation purposes but contravenes another. For example, the Treasury rule indicates it might disallow a deduction where farmland protection is contemplated by delineated government policy but "a significant naturally occurring ecosystem could be injured or destroyed by the use of pesticides in the operation of the farm."[28]

Other forms of poor stewardship, including abusive cropping of highly erodible fields or natural wetlands (Chapter 3), should likewise disqualify easement donations of farmland. Much of the obligation to prevent such environmental inconsistency must fall

---

* In comments on the proposed Treasury rule, (see chapter note 19, at D-14-17), conservationists cautioned that this illustration could mislead easement donors and the IRS into an overly narrow view of allowable farmland conservation easements. The commenters urged, but did not obtain, addition of more generic language affirming the importance of conserving farmlands' food and fiber production capability.

to land trusts and other prospective easement recipients who, to a greater degree than the IRS, have the expertise to recognize conflicts among conservation purposes.

Retirement of Eroding Cropland. Easements may also be useful in withdrawing severely eroding farmland from crop production. As contemplated in the 1985 Food Security Act's Conservation Reserve Program, reversion to perennial grass, tree or shrub cover may be the only effective conservation strategy where even heroic abatement measures cannot forestall lost productivity or off-site damage from soil erosion. Cropland retirement also can mitigate water pollution; vegetative buffers have proved highly effective in preventing eroded sediment and farm chemicals from reaching streams and lakes adjoining cropland.[29]

Conceivably, a property owner who donates an erosion control easement could give up the right to raise annual crops but retain the right to conduct more sustainable economic pursuits such as livestock grazing, tree farming, maintenance of wildlife habitat or commercial recreation. In such a case, the landowner could deduct the difference between the field's market value as cropland and its value under a less intensive management regime.

Such a transition could even help lend economic stability to rural communities. A recent study at the University of Missouri concluded that an easement program structured for erosion control and commodity surplus reduction could have favorable results for the Midwest:

> ...the output mix [of farms in the Midwest] would be more toward livestock and less grain sales than in the past. In the process, employment opportunities could be expected to be maintained and, in some areas and industries, even enhanced ... Also, this community stabilization ... would strengthen the rural economy during a difficult transition period. Finally, allowing commercial use of [conservation easement program] land makes good economic sense if the enrolled land can profitably produce forage or timber rather than lie idle and generate little or no social product.[30]

In the right circumstances, easements shifting eroding cropland to less intensive use should satisfy the Revenue Code's requirements. As to the government policy test, there are many statutory articulations of the public interest in erosion control including, as noted, the conservation title of the 1985 Food Security Act. It should be particularly helpful to prospective donors that the Act's erosion control language applies to a discrete category of "highly erodible" cropland identified by standard technical criteria based on the potential for soil degradation.[31]

Some state and local provisions may also be helpful in establishing "clearly delineated" government policy favoring retirement of eroding cropland. Iowa, for example, has a strict soil conservation law on the books. As noted in Chapter 3, Wisconsin and other states have adopted "T by 2000" programs affirming a commitment to reduce erosion to tolerable rates by the turn of the century. Several counties in eastern Colorado have enacted ordinances to penalize destructive sodbusting of fragile rangeland.

With respect to the public benefit test, the Treasury regulation indicates that the test may be satisfied by "consistency of the proposed open space use with public programs (whether federal, state, or local) for conservation in the region, including programs for ... water quality maintenance or enhancement ... [or for] erosion control."[32] Additional public benefits of a cropland retirement easement that often may be cited include the creation of critical wildlife habitat and reduced farm surplus.

In addition, it may be possible for some landowners to bypass the open space requirements and qualify land retirement for an easement deduction to protect "relatively natural habitat ... [for] fish, wildlife, or plants."[33] For example, the re-creation of native prairie on eroding Corn Belt cropland or reclamation of wetland environments should satisfy the test. Unlike "open space" easements, "natural habitat" easements presumably would have to proscribe or impose major restrictions on livestock grazing, timber production or other commercial uses of the property.

Groundwater Protection. Conservation easements also have the potential to protect rural groundwater. In each instance, site conditions would dictate the needed adjustments to agricultural practices, but easements could specify, for example, the sealing of contaminated agricultural drainage wells. On many farm fields in the Midwest, wells installed to enable intensive corn and soybean production on fertile, wet soils now act as conduits transporting sediment, bacteria, fertilizer nitrates and chemical pesticides to groundwater.[34] Where the primary pollution conduits are natural topographic sinkholes, as prevalent in "karst" regions featuring porous limestone geology, easements might specify changes in tillage, irrigation practices or fertilizer and pesticide use.

As noted, the Treasury rule cites consistency with efforts to maintain or enhance water quality as an indication of "significant public benefit." This language might be helpful to prospective donors, as might evidence of state and local laws concerned with water quality. Some groundwater protection easements might even qualify as protection of "natural habitat" where they enable beneficial reversion to native vegetation and environments such as wetlands.

Easements might operate to conserve the supply as well as the quality of groundwater. For example, farmers could receive tax deductions for donation of easements restricting irrigation where pumping from agricultural wells is causing irreversible aquifer depletion or serious intermittent harm to local water tables.

Proposals for Strengthening Tax Benefits for Easements

Section 170(h) was enacted as part of the Tax Treatment Extension Act of 1980,[35] a law that modified and extended authority in place since the mid-1970s.[36] The Senate Finance Committee, which crafted the 1980 legislation, observed "that the preservation of our country's natural resources and cultural heritage is important, and ... that conservation easements now play an important role in preservation efforts."[37] Similar language appeared in the companion report from the House Ways and Means Committee.[38]

As noted, taxpayers qualifying under section 170(h) may deduct from taxable income the value of the easements, calculated as the difference in property value before and after imposition of easement restrictions.[39] The amount of the resulting tax benefits is a function of the taxpayer's financial situation.

For example, a taxpayer in today's 28 percent bracket who donates an easement worth $50,000 could realize a $14,000 benefit ($50,000 x 28%). In this case, the public would get a bargain, having acquired conservation values worth $50,000 for just a little more than one-fourth that amount in forgone revenue.

Although easement deductions have proven highly valuable for conservation, a number of concerns and problems have arisen concerning the implementation of section 170(h).

Monitoring and Enforcement of Section 170(h). Within the 1980 Tax Treatment Extension Act, Congress directed the Treasury Department to issue an evaluation of section 170(h). The Department's report, published in December 1987,[40] affirmed the rationale for the section as similar to that for other charitable contributions, stating that an easement donation "may provide public benefits above and beyond any potential gain to the owner."[41]

The Department gave the provision less than a ringing endorsement, however. The report contends that the current system presents thorny administrative problems for the Internal Revenue Service and opens the door to abuse by persons who, through easement donations, may reap more economic benefits than society at large.[42] The Department concluded that "some combination of direct government purchases of easements and government grants to nonprofit organizations for the purpose of purchasing easements may provide a more efficient means of land preservation and allow greater public benefit than the current policy of deductibility."[43]

The primary administrative problem is valuation, which often requires speculation about the worth of various rights inherent in property ownership that are not traded frequently on the open market. In many cases, it may prove difficult for the IRS to detect fraudulent appraisals that exaggerate easement values. To an extent, this problem is common to all noncash charitable contributions.[44]

However, the Treasury report acknowledges the absence of any reliable data confirming that excessive valuation has been a serious problem since the tax code began to allow easement deductibility.[45] In the absence of more persuasive data to the contrary, the potential for abuse should be addressed not by abandoning section 170(h) but by closer IRS scrutiny of large noncash donations in general, including those for conservation easements.[46] Given the need for financially efficient methods of achieving conservation in today's fiscal climate, elimination of the tax deduction would be a serious mistake.

On a related issue, the Treasury report argues persuasively for rigorous long-term monitoring and enforcement of conservation easement restrictions, recognizing that violations undercut the public's tax-supported investment in conservation. This is consistent with recommendations issued by the Land Trust Exchange, a national clearinghouse for land trust organizations, in connection with the Exchange's national survey in 1985.[47]

This recommendation is sound although, in practice, violations appear to be the exception to the rule. Responding to the Land Trust Exchange survey, only 13 percent of government program administrators and five percent of private program administrators reported violations of easement terms.[48] One helpful check is that donors must now furnish the IRS with documentation showing that easements have been recorded on deeds to property.[49] As the Treasury Department has observed, "This will ensure that future owners are bound by the restrictions and that donors do not receive deductions based on a gift in perpetuity for donations that are, in fact, of short duration."[50]

The Problem of Appreciated Value. Where property has appreciated in value, an easement donor benefits both from the charitable deduction and by reducing the amount of the capital gain that will be realized whenever the property is sold. This is true not only for easements but for all contributions of appreciated property.

Pursuant to the 1986 Tax Reform Act, this double advantage is no longer available to those taxpayers subject to the Alternative Minimum Tax,[51] a provision designed to ensure that persons with high incomes pay their fair share of taxes notwithstanding allowable deductions and credits. The minimum tax is calculated at a lower rate than that normally applicable to taxpayers in upper income brackets; however it disallows many deductions categorized as "preference items."[52]

Any easement donation made by a taxpayer subject to the alternative minimum tax is now limited to the person's "basis" (usually calculated from the original purchase price) in the donated property rights; the appreciated portion is a taxable preference item. Although it is too early to assess fully the 1986 provision's impact on charitable giving, the reform may be deterring some donors from making gifts of conservation easements.* This especially may be true for prospective easement donors who are subject to alternative minimum taxation and have held their purchased property through long inflationary periods.

By taxing appreciated property value at the time of donation, the alternative minimum tax cuts against general tax rules. Normally, federal income tax is imposed "only on transactions ... not on the mere enrichment of a property owner" who does not realize gain from an appreciating asset until the asset is sold.[53] Gains are generally not considered realized (and hence are not taxed) upon a gift and are never taxed as income upon the death of the property owner. In requiring that the gain be taxed merely because the easement is donated to charity, the law perversely encourages the taxpayer to forgo donation and retain full ownership of the affected property. Congress should remove this disincentive for charitable giving by reinstating appreciated value deductions for alternative minimum taxpayers.

Estate and Gift Taxation. Conservation easement donations can reduce considerably estate and gift, as well as income, tax liabilities. This occurs because estate appraisals are lowered by the value of donated easements. The basic mechanism is illustrated in the following example developed by Thomas Coughlin, a specialist in the taxation of conservation easements:

---

* Another way in which the Tax Reform Act reduced the value of charitable contribution deductions was through a general lowering of marginal tax rates, particularly the drop in the top bracket from 50 percent to 28 percent. A story in the January 26, 1988 *Wall Street Journal* titled "Tax Changes Hit Groups in Land Conservation" reported that the tax rate reduction has had a chilling effect on donations of land, and presumably easements, to non-profit organizations.

Broadly stated, decedents dying after 1988 with taxable estates greater than $2,500,000 will be taxed at the maximum estate tax rate of 50 percent. Thus, a decedent with an estate valued at $10,000,000 can expect to pay a significant portion of that amount in Federal estate taxes. If the bulk of the decedent's estate is held in a single large landholding, it will be necessary to sell some or all of the land to satisfy anticipated $4,000,000 to $5,000,000 in Federal estate taxes.

The gift of an easement valued at $4,000,000 would reduce the value of the decedent's estate from $10,000,000 to $6,000,000, thereby reducing the estate tax burden from almost $5,000,000 to around $2,000,000. Although an easement gift, by itself, would not protect the land against forced sale, it does reduce the estate tax burden by approximately 60 percent and increases the chance that the family can continue to retain ownership of the property. If the family does not want to retain continued ownership, the easement insures that the land will be protected in perpetuity.[54]

This scenario can carry a risk, however, in the form of a sizable unanticipated estate or gift tax burden in the event that the IRS rules against a claimed section 170(h) income tax deduction after an estate has passed to an heir or donee. This is significant because "in terms of land conservation even a remote threat of transfer tax has a chilling effect on the conservation efforts of governmental agencies and private non-profit organizations."[55]

An attempt was made to address this problem in section 1422 of the 1986 Tax Reform Act. That provision deleted, for estate and gift tax purposes, the four specific criteria under which an easement may qualify for a "conservation purpose" deduction. Apparently, the intent was to assure that rigid requirements would not be applied after donations had been made in anticipation of deductibility; House and Senate conferees stated the changes should allow "gift or estate tax deductions to be claimed for qualified conservation contributions without regard to whether the contribution satisfies the income tax conservation purpose requirement."[56]

Whether this result was accomplished is unclear, since section 1422 did not repeal the more general language requiring that an easement be "exclusively for conservation purposes" in order to qualify. Presumably, the IRS and the courts could continue to apply some criteria and, if appropriate, disqualify some donations to assure that the basic intent of the law was met. This uncertainty needs to be clarified.*

The Need for Complementary Incentives

For all its merit, the Revenue Code is not always effective as an inducement to the use of conservation easements. Some landowners are not in a financial position to take advantage of an income tax deduction. Moreover, tax benefits will rarely offset completely the value of the property rights given up. As a result, complementary incentives are necessary; recommendations on two mechanisms with significance for agriculture are set forth below.

Easements for Farm Credit Relief. Among the farmers least likely to benefit from tax deductions are those who suffer from chronic financial shortfalls and extraordinarily high ratios of debts to assets.[57] This category includes many debt-ridden producers who are unable to repay money borrowed from the Farmers Home Administration (FmHA), a "lender of last resort" within USDA that provides funds to farmers unable to obtain credit from banks or other commercial sources.

Section 1318 of the 1985 Food Security Act[58] provides authority for delinquent FmHA borrowers to grant conservation easements to the federal government in exchange for partial debt forgiveness. In particular, the law authorizes FmHA to acquire easements for conservation, wildlife or recreation purposes on environmentally sensitive lands used as collateral to secure farmers' loans. The easement term must be a minimum of 50 years.**

---

* The problem may be ameliorated somewhat if the IRS successfully implements and extends Rev. Proc. 88-50, which was adopted for a one-year test in late 1988. Under this new procedure, the agency apparently intends to consider requests from living taxpayers for a ruling on all estate tax issues except tax computation, actuarial factors and factual issues such as fair market value.

** In addition, pursuant to the "sodbuster" and "swampbuster" provisions of the Food Security Act, no FmHA loan proceeds may be used for destructive plowing of highly erodible fields and natural wetlands. Enacting a multi-billion
(continued...)

Unfortunately, as of early 1989, FmHA has yet to take a conservation easement to restructure a delinquent debt. It is to be hoped that this situation will change in the wake of a regulation promulgated in 1988 implementing section 1318. The rule elevates conservation easements to a "primary loan service program" designed to restructure bad debts and keep farmers from facing foreclosure.[59] Based on the recommendations of interagency review teams, FmHA has indicated it will accept easements on wetlands, highly erodible land and certain "upland" with environmental significance, provided the land was cropped in each of the three years prior to the enactment of the Food Security Act in 1985.

FmHA should also implement section 1314 of the Food Security Act, which gives the administration discretion to grant or sell conservation easements on "inventory" land that the agency has obtained as a result of loan foreclosure.[60] In addition, a complementary provision in the 1987 Agricultural Credit Act (§616) enables FmHA to convey conservation easements without reimbursement "to any Federal or State Agency" on certain inventory land that "has marginal value for agricultural production, is environmentally sensitive, or has special management importance."[61] This provision too should be implemented aggressively.

Direct Purchase of Easements. Various state and local governments have also achieved significant conservation results in agriculture by direct purchase of easements from landowners. A noteworthy example of this is the landmark Reinvest in Minnesota (RIM) program created in 1986. Similar in concept to the federal conservation reserve program, RIM seeks long-term retirement of marginal and ecologically sensitive cropland. Qualifying farmers may obtain direct payments in exchange for

---

**(...continued)

dollar "bailout" package to rescue the ailing Farm Credit System (FCS), a network of lending institutions that holds one-third of the nation's farm debt, Congress in 1988 rejected a proposal to apply similar restrictions to FCS loans. The restrictions should be reconsidered the next time Congress revisits farm credit legislation.

either a 20-year or permanent easement term,[62] but payments are significantly greater for permanent easements.[63]*

A second example comprises the "purchase of development rights" programs described in Chapter 5 and currently administered by six states and eight local jurisdictions, all but one in the East. Under these programs, state and local governments buy easements proscribing development that would convert farmland to nonagricultural uses.

Other state and local governments would do well to imitate these models. Land retirement programs patterned after RIM might benefit the Chesapeake Bay region, for example, where the federal conservation reserve has failed to attract much participation. Similarly, states and local communities in the Midwest and other major agricultural regions should consider purchase of development rights programs similar to those that have worked well in the East to stem the loss of prime farmland at the urban fringe.

In addition, the federal government should develop easement purchase programs that complement those of the states. As noted, the U.S. Fish and Wildlife Service has established an impressive track record for protecting natural wetland habitat. The Service's easement programs could serve as a model for other federal endeavors such as the purchase of cropping rights on erosion-prone farm fields.

Finally, there are several methods by which the federal government might influence the use of conservation easements to serve high-priority objectives. Purchase programs administered by federal agencies could authorize direct payments for a portion of the fair market value of designated easements, with the balance left tax deductible. In such cases, there should be no question as to whether the claimed easement deduction satisfied the relevant tests under section 170(h).

---

* In 1986, roughly 21,000 acres were enrolled in RIM, with approximately 10 percent of that total committed to permanent easement; another estimated 10,000 acres entered the program in 1987, with some 60 percent of these lands retired permanently from crop production. A small but significant portion–approximately 1,200 acres–of the 1987 total are for restoration of agriculturally converted wetlands.

Chapter Notes

1. *See* T. Coughlin and T. Plaut, "Less-than-fee Acquisition for the Preservation of Open Space: Does it Work?" 44 *Journal of the American Institute of Planning* (Oct. 1978).

2. T. Barrett and P. Livermore, *The Conservation Easement in California* 4 (1983).

3. S. Hinchman, "The Fine Art of Infiltrage," 20 *High Country News* 8-13 (Apr. 25, 1988).

4. American Farmland Trust, "American Farmland: New Hope for an American Heritage," 10 (1987 Annual Report).

5. B. Emory, "Land Trusts: A Key Link in the Conservation Chain," 20 *Parks and Recreation* 46 (Nov. 1985).

6. K. Barton, "Federal Fish and Wildlife Agency Budgets," in *Audubon Wildlife Report 1987* 349 (1987).

7. J. Mertes, "Trends in Land Use," 20 *Parks and Recreation* 46 (May 1985).

8. Land Trust Exchange, *Report on 1985 National Survey of Government and Non-Profit Easement Programs* 7 (Dec. 1985).

9. Maryland Environmental Trust, *To Preserve a Heritage: Conservation Easements* 7 (1987).

10. K. Hambrick, "Charitable Donations of Conservation Easements: Valuation, Enforcement and Public Benefit," 59 *Taxes* 347 (June 1981).

11. I.R.C. §170(h)(l).

12. *Id.* §170(h)(4)(A).

13. Income Taxes, Qualified Conservation Contributions, 26 C.F.R. Parts 1, 20, 25 and 602, 51 Fed. Reg. 1496-1507 (Jan. 14, 1986).

14. 26 C.F.R. §1.170A-14(d)(4)(iii)(A).

15. *Id.* §1.170A-14(d)(4)(iv).

16. *Id.* §1.170A-14(d)(4)(vi)(A).

17. *See* D. Sand, "A New Farm Easement Program," 6 *American Land Forum Magazine* 9-11 (Winter 1986).

18. D. Sand, "Conservation Easements and the Conservation Movement," 40 *Journal of Soil and Water Conservation* 337 (July-Aug. 1985).

19. S. Small, *The Federal Tax Law of Conservation Easements* 6-4 (1986).

20. *Id.* at 10-4.

21. 26 C.F.R. §1.170A-14(d)(4)(iii)(A).

22. *See* K. Grillo and D. Seid, *State Laws Relating to Preferential Assessment of Farmland* 4 (USDA-ERS Staff Report No. AGES870326) (June 1987). *See* Chapter 5 for a discussion of preferential taxation generally.

23. *See* 26 C.F.R. §1.170A-14(d)(4)(iv).

24. Small, *supra* note 19, at 10-4.

25. I.R.C. §170(h)(4)(iii)(1).

26. 26 C.F.R. §1.70A-14(d)(4)(ii).

27. I.R.C. §170(h)(1)(c).

28. 26 C.F.R. §1.70A-14(e)(2).

29. *See, e.g.*, U.S. Environmental Protection Agency, *Setting Priorities: The Key to Nonpoint Source Control* 28 (July 1987).

30. D. Ervin *et al.*, "Conservation Easements: An Integrated Policy Approach to Soil Erosion Control and Agricultural Supply Management," 150 (University of Missouri - Columbia) (Feb. 25, 1987).

31. *See* 7 C.F.R. §12.21. As detailed in USDA regulations, land is "highly erodible" if it meets or exceeds a value of eight on an erosion potential index that ranges from zero (low) to fifteen (high). This definition describes approximately 118 million acres (28 percent) of the nation's cropland base.

32. 26 C.F.R. §1.170A-14(d)(4)(iv)(3).

33. I.R.C. §170(h)(4)(a)(ii).

34. *See* C. Cramer, "Iowa Taxes Chemicals to Protect Groundwater," 10 *The New Farm* 22-23 (Feb. 1988).

35.   Tax Treatment Extension Act, Pub. L. No. 96-541, §6, 94 Stat. 3204, 3206-3208 (1980).

36.   Tax Reform Act of 1976, Pub. L. No. 94-455, 90 Stat. 1520, as amended by Tax Reduction and Simplification Act of 1977, Pub. L. No. 95-30, 91 Stat. 126. *See also* R. Dunford, "An Overview of Federal Tax Policies Encouraging Donations of Conservation Easements to Preserve Natural Areas," 9-15 (Congressional Research Service Report No. 84-48 ENR) (Feb. 29, 1984).

37.   S. Rep. No. 1007, 96th Cong., 2d Sess. 17 (Sept. 30, 1980).

38.   H.R. Rep. No. 1279, 96th Cong., 2d Sess. 31 (Sept. 4, 1980).

39.   For an excellent summary of the "before and after" method of easement valuation, *see Appraising Easements* 19-23 (National Trust for Historic Preservation and Land Trust Exchange) (Oct. 1984).

40.   U.S. Department of the Treasury, "A Report to Congress on the Use of Tax Deductions for Donations of Conservation Easements" (Dec. 18, 1987).

41.   *Id.* at 8.

42.   *Id.* at 10-12.

43.   *Id.* at 2.

44.   *Id.*

45.   *Id.* at 11.

46.   *Id.* at 12.

47.   Land Trust Exchange, *supra* note 8, at 20.

48.   *Id.* at 13.

49.   Treasury report, *supra* note 40, at 13.

50.   *Id.*

51.   Tax Reform Act of 1986, Pub. L. No. 99-514, §701, 100 Stat. 2085, 2320-2345 (amending I.R.C. §57).

52.   *See generally* U.S. Department of the Treasury, Internal Revenue Service, *Alternative Minimum Tax* (I.R.S. Publication 909) (Nov. 1986).

53. R. Rice and L. Solomon, *Federal Income Taxation* 90 (1979). These authors are somewhat critical of this general rule, stating that "[t]he realization requirement constitutes a deferral of taxation ... Even if the gain is ultimately taxed to the original owner at ordinary income rates, the taxpayer receives something of value as a result of the deferral of tax."

54. T. Coughlin, "Tax Consequences of Charitable Contributions of Easements in Income, Estate and Gift Tax Planning After Tax Reform Act of 1986," 5 (memo) (Nov. 19, 1987). Pursuant to the Revenue Act of 1987, enacted after publication of this memo, the maximum estate tax rate will be 55 percent through 1993.

55. Letter from Kingsbury Browne to Joint Committee on Taxation 2 (Jan. 27, 1987).

56. H.R. Rep. No. 841, 99th Cong., 2d Sess. II-772 (1986).

57. In 1985, a USDA estimate placed approximately 11 percent of the nation's farmers in this category. D. Harrington and T. Carlin, *The U.S. Farm Sector: How Is It Weathering the 1980's?* v (USDA-ERS Agriculture Information Bulletin No. 506) (Apr. 1987).

58. Food Security Act of 1985, Pub. L. No. 99-198, §1318, 99 Stat. 1354, 1530, 1531 7 U.S.C. §1997.

59. *See* USDA Farmers Home Administration, Exhibit H–Primary Loan Service Programs (Farm Debt Restructure and Conservation Easements), 53 Fed. Reg. 35,750 - 35,753 (Sept. 14, 1988).

60. *Id.* §1314, 99 Stat. 1526-1528, 7 U.S.C. §1985.

61. *See* H. R. Rep. No. 490, 100th Cong., 1st Sess. 120 (1987) (Conference Report on H.R. 3030, The Agricultural Credit Act of 1987).

62. Background for this discussion was furnished by Wayne Edgerton, R.I.M. Reserve Coordinator for the Minnesota Department of Agriculture's Soil and Water Conservation Board.

63. RIM payments for permanent easements are the lesser of projected cash rent for farming the land in perpetuity or 90 percent of local prevailing farmland prices. Payments for twenty year easements are always 65 percent of the calculated permanent easement values. In either case, the farmers may elect to receive the money as a lump sum or in equal installments spread over several years. As of early 1988, the cost to the Minnesota Treasury had been approximately $13.9 million.

7

Private Forestry–Taxing The Tree Farm

Much of the nation's privately owned forestland is held by farmers. More active management of such nonindustrial private forests (NIPFs) could relieve pressure for commercial logging of public lands, including the federally owned national forests. Increased NIPF management also could, with proper environmental precautions, help conserve fragile farmland and help abate the global warming trend. Unfortunately, tax disincentives and other barriers stand in the way.

The Untapped Potential of Private Forestry

Nearly three-fourths of all commercial timberland in the United States, some 347 million acres, is privately owned (Figure 3). The majority of this private forest land–80 percent–is held by nonindustrial owners,* with most of the remainder in the hands of large corporations.[1] Nonindustrial private holdings include 30 percent of the country's growing stock of softwood timber and 70 percent of its hardwood stock.[2] NIPF owners vary widely in age, primary occupation and tenure,[3] but the largest share of their lands, about 97 million acres, is held by farmers.[4]

A sizable fraction of all NIPF land holds significant potential for more active management. On approximately 70 million acres of nonindustrial private forests, planting trees on nonstocked areas, replacement of low-value trees with marketable species, and stand maintenance procedures such as thinning could increase net annual timber growth by 3.7 billion cubic feet.[5] This would satisfy more than half the increase in demand for wood the government projects will be realized by 2020.[6]

---

* "Nonindustrial" timber owners do not own or operate timber processing facilities.

Figure 3

Ownership of U.S. Commercial Timberland

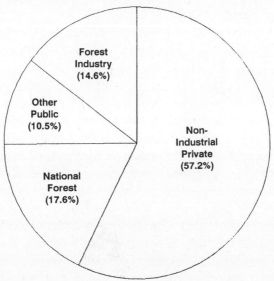

Source: USDA, *Forest Statistics of the United States* (1987). "Commercial" timberland is defined by USDA as land that can produce at least 20 cubic feet of wood per acre per year and is not reserved from timber harvest.

This is especially true in the South, where about 70 percent of the productive timberland is in nonindustrial ownership.[7] A recent USDA estimate projects that more than 50 million acres of southern nonindustrial forests could be managed to produce an additional 2.3 billion cubic feet of wood per year. Moreover, these impressive numbers are conservative, based only on those lands and practices capable of yielding an annual return for timber growers of at least four percent above inflation.[8]

Environmental Benefits

Increased commercial wood production from NIPF lands, if attained in an environmentally sound manner, could reduce pressure on public forests to meet the nation's increasing wood demand. This benefit would be significant because public forests, unlike their private counterparts, have been established by law partly to provide amenities that can conflict with commercial logging. The federally owned national forests, for example, attract approximately 225 million recreation visitor-days each year, far more than any other category of federal lands, including the national parks.[9]

Forest recreation visits will probably increase in the next few decades as the population becomes younger, wealthier and more recreation-oriented.[10] Moreover, experts in the field predict that, of all forms of outdoor recreation, experiences requiring remote, undisturbed forest will rise most quickly in popularity.[11]

In addition to recreation, public forests are valuable for other important amenity values. More than half of all surface water in the 11 western states originates in headwater streams on the national forests.[12] Public forests also host abundant wildlife, including species that do not exist elsewhere in the United States.[13]

Public forests are generally better suited than private lands to maintain amenity values. Half the nation's private forestland is distributed in individual parcels of less than 500 acres and cannot furnish large tracts of contiguous remote forest necessary to the survival of many wildlife species.[14] Neither can private forests, with their restricted access and smaller acreage, be expected to absorb increases in demand for primitive recreation. The maintenance of scarce public lands for these values is particularly important in the East, where national forests constitute only four percent of the total forested land base.[15]

This will only become more difficult if, as projected, demand for wood increases. USDA's Forest Service has estimated that, by 2040, wood demand could increase more than 40 percent above the 1986 level.[16] If the national forests are forced to maintain their current share of the market, their annual harvest could increase by more than one billion cubic feet in the next 40 years.[17]

Some likely effects of this scenario are becoming more apparent as the Forest Service completes a new generation of management plans for each of the 156 national forests. The 107 draft or final plans released by the agency as of early 1987 would increase the aggregate timber cut by more than 72 percent and, astoundingly, construct an additional 200,000 miles of logging roads to accommodate projected increases in wood demand.[18] Such a course could seriously harm basic forest values, causing damage to water quality and fisheries, wildlife habitat and scenic vistas.[19]

Besides reducing pressure for more logging on public forests, an increase in sustained private forestry could encourage tree planting and help stem damage from intensive annual crop production on fragile farmlands. In the recent past, transformation of forests on fragile land to cropland has been a cause of serious soil erosion and consequent pollution of streams and waterways by sediment and farm chemicals.[20] Nationwide, USDA has identified approximately 40 million acres of forestland as having a medium or high potential for additional conversion to intensive rowcrop production.[21]

Fortunately for private forestry, there are incentives for reversing this trend in the 1985 Food Security Act's Conservation Reserve Program.[22] In particular, the law specifies that at least one-eighth of the 45 million acres targeted for long-term conservation contracts under the reserve are to be planted with trees. This goal unfortunately has not come close to fulfillment but, by the reserve program's sixth enrollment in February 1988, 1.5 million acres had been dedicated to trees, primarily in the South.[23] USDA estimated in 1987 that the program accounted for up to 70 percent of the new tree planting on NIPF lands.[24]

Environmental Risks

Enticing as the benefits of private forestry are, they could be overshadowed by environmental damage if improper practices are employed in more active timber management. The need for care is particularly acute when "clearcut" logging regimes, which remove all trees in a given area, are employed.[25] Another frequent cause of damage is improper construction of logging roads and skid trails to gain access to stands for cutting and removal.[26]

Among problems related to logging, perhaps the most obvious is visual degradation, especially on slopes or lands visible from popular transportation routes. Clearcutting has been referred to a an "aesthetic disaster."[27] Generally, the public prefers natural-appearing stands and responds negatively to cutover "slash," stumps and bare soil.[28] The noise of logging and road construction and general disruption associated with large-scale commercial activity in rural areas also can be significant.

Less obviously but especially pervasive are the effects on the biologic diversity of forests, especially when essential wildlife habitat is destroyed. For example, while clearcutting large areas may be favorable in the short term for certain species such as deer, it is detrimental over time to others. In particular, ecologists fault excessive logging and related forest development for the continued endangerment of such species as the red-cockaded woodpecker and northern spotted owl.[29] In Canada and upper New England, switching from selective harvest methods to clearcutting contributed to significant reduction in populations of trout, deer, caribou and elk.[30]

Aquatic habitat is also vulnerable to logging activities, which can cause siltation and nutrient leaching and remove shade trees that maintain favorable stream temperatures.[31] In places, improper use of clearcutting has increased annual sediment yields by more than 100 times the levels found on undisturbed watersheds.[32] The result of such damage can be the elimination of important fish species from a waterway.

These problems are exacerbated by lack of reforestation, one of the most significant environmental shortcomings of nonindustrial private forestry as currently practiced. According to one USDA Assistant Secretary, for example, only approximately 60 percent of harvested nonindustrial pine lands in the South now undergo reforestation.[33] Although this represents encouraging progress from the 1970s—when the comparable figure was a dismal 46 percent—the current situation is far from a complete solution.

Fortunately, environmental problems on private forests often can be avoided or reduced significantly through the use of proper management practices. In particular, the use of vegetative buffer strips around waterways, careful road construction and selective harvest of single trees or small groups can do much to lessen the visual impacts of logging, prevent watershed and soil damage, enhance tree regeneration and protect wildlife habitat.[34]

The key is careful tailoring of practices to individual site characteristics.*

Of course, even with effective mitigation, an appropriate harmony that achieves increases in both timber production and environmental protection may be difficult to attain. Reconciling the two interests is far easier, however, on private lands than on public lands where citizen rights and expectations for noncommercial benefits are greater. Environmentally responsible, sustained forestry on private lands has much to recommend it to both the public and the landowner.

Barriers to Private Forestry

If sustained private forestry is such a good idea, why is there not more of it? Unfortunately, many economic and practical considerations tend to discourage increased participation by NIPF landowners.

One important economic impediment is the inherent lack of liquidity associated with private forestry. Unlike most businesses, including most agricultural crop production, the realization of revenue from timber harvesting is not an annual event. Instead, the growth of commercially viable trees from seedlings may require 40 years or more. In the interim, owners may lack funds for site preparation, tree planting, stand thinning and other beneficial business practices.[35]

The long-term nature of the enterprise also introduces an exceptional degree of risk for the owner. It is difficult at best to predict markets for wood products decades in advance. In addition, at any point in the growing cycle portions of tree crops or even an entire investment can be lost due to capricious events of weather, insects, tree disease or fire.[36] Federal agricultural subsidy programs traditionally have been justified as protecting farmers against the vagaries of weather and other risks of crop production, but they generally do not extend to woodland owners.

---

* Conservation-oriented foresters such as Leon Minckler and Walton Smith have written eloquently about environmentally sensitive private forest management.

Still another set of difficulties is posed by the small size, around 70 acres on the average,[37] of most individual NIPF holdings. Smaller tracts cannot take advantage of so-called economies of scale and, on a per-acre basis, face higher costs, lower revenues and higher risks than do larger holdings.* The average per-acre cost of silvicultural treatments on 20-acre lots, for example, is about double that on tracts larger than 100 acres.[38]

In addition, it can require more effort to mitigate environmentally harmful impacts of harvesting small ownerships. On larger holdings, portions can more easily be left intact without sacrificing financial gain. Researchers have found that, in general, smaller forest tracts are managed less intensively for wood production than their larger counterparts.[39]

Compounding the economic disincentives, many NIPF owners lack sufficient technical expertise to manage their lands on a sustained, productive basis. For example, one survey found that nonindustrial pine forest owners failed to reforest more than half their clearcut acres largely on the mistaken belief that marketable pine stands would regenerate naturally.[40] Lack of familiarity with environmentally sound forest practices is also common. This is particularly significant, given that many owners acquire and hold their forests partly for noncommercial reasons including residence, recreation, personal enjoyment and hunting.[41]

Finally, many NIPF owners lack access to reliable timber market information and, as a result, fail to offer their timber at competitive prices.[42] Although most states do not have regular timber price reporting services, both timber offerings and unit prices received appear to be higher where such services exist.[43]

Public Forestry Programs

For decades, the federal government and the states have sought to address these problems through a variety of programs. For the most part, these have been helpful to landowners but also plagued with budgetary and administrative problems.

---

* While circumstances vary, many experts consider 50 acres a minimum threshold for a forestland owner to begin realizing economies of scale.

In particular, USDA's Forest Service, through its State and Private Forestry branch, is nominally structured to provide assistance to NIPF owners. The branch's Cooperative Forestry Program provides technical and financial support for improved forest resource management, utilization, protection, and planning on nonfederal forest lands.* Another USDA effort, the Forestry Incentives Program, provides landowners with cost-share assistance for site preparation, tree planting and stand improvement practices.[44]

State governments provide much of the administration for these federal efforts and, in addition, nearly all provide some sort of education and technical assistance through state foresters or comparable officials and their staffs. Most state programs are directed at activities such as timber management, water quality protection, reforestation and forest protection, and wildlife and aesthetic management.[45] A few provide their own cost-share programs for tree planting and timber stand improvement.[46]

These are popular services. In 1987, for example, the U.S. Forest Service and state foresters developed management plans covering 4.3 million acres of NIPF lands.[47] In the same year, 1,098,946 acres of private land received reforestation assistance, and 240,180 acres received assistance in improving timber quality.[48]

In general, the payoff associated with public programs that reach NIPF owners is substantial. Summarizing a large body of research, Dr. Frederick Cubbage of the University of Georgia reported in 1987 that technical assistance tends to increase the probability of harvest and regeneration, price received per unit of timber, and present value per acre of forest holdings.[49] It has been estimated 60 percent of the decisions to reforest harvested NIPF lands are influenced by technical and cost-share assistance from federal or state foresters.[50] Moreover, Cubbage reported the findings of at least two researchers indicating that public forestry assistance pays off literally in the form of increased income tax revenue to public treasuries.[51]

---

* Other State and Private Forestry programs administered by the Forest Service include Cooperative Fire Protection, Forest Pest Management, and Human Resources.

These programs, however, extend to only a small portion of NIPF lands. Currently, the federal government is assisting owners of only one percent of the country's 347 million acres of private forestland. Even the most active state assistance programs, those in the South, reach only between one and two percent of NIPF owners and between one and two percent of NIPF land.[52] As for the education component, there are only an estimated 200 forestry and related resource personnel employed by all government extension services in the country.[53]

Moreover, the budget trends are unfavorable. Within the Forest Service's relatively modest budget for State and Private Forestry, the portion devoted to Cooperative Forestry dropped from nearly one-third of the total to less than 20 percent from 1979 to 1985. Cooperative Forestry programs focusing on NIPF owners have been the most seriously curtailed; they were halved between 1979 and 1985.[54] Funding for the Forestry Incentives Program has declined 64 percent in constant dollars since the program's inception. In all, programs providing assistance to private forestry currently constitute only about three percent of the Forest Service's budget, even while attempting to provide services to 57 percent of the nation's forestland base.[55]

State programs, often directly affected by a shortage of federal money, have suffered their own financial crises.* Large cuts have been reported for several state forestry budgets,[56] and state foresters overwhelmingly indicate a need for expansion of their technical assistance and education efforts.[57]

The Impact of the Tax Code

Historically, the federal tax code has contained a number of income tax benefits for timber producers. Prior to the 1986 Tax

---

* Public forestry assistance programs pale before their agricultural counterparts. Budgets for the Soil Conservation Service's technical assistance program and the Agricultural Stabilization and Conservation Service's cost-share assistance program totaled more than $450 million in Fiscal Year 1986, almost seven times the Forest Service's State and Private Forestry expenditures for that year. Also in Fiscal Year 1986, direct federal payments for forestry assistance amounted to less than two-tenths of one percent of direct payments to crop growers under USDA's commodity programs. Forestry payments totaled slightly more than $15 million; commodity payments totaled nearly $9 billion.

Reform Act, preferential capital gains treatment was among the most favorable. As discussed in Chapter 2, pre-1986 law allowed the exclusion from taxation of 60 percent of net income derived from the sale of capital assets, including timber, held for six months or more. The capital gains preference was not available, however, for most other farm crops.

This tax preference for timber sales was at least in part a conservation-driven policy.[58] Before 1944, capital gains treatment had been allowed for timber only if timber had been held as an investment *per se* rather than as part of an ongoing trade or business. To qualify, timber could not have been held for sale to customers, and all standing timber had to be sold at once in a "lump sum" sale. As a result, owners liquidated timber holdings through one-time clearcuts and neglected reforestation and sustained management. Selective cuts and long-term forestry were, in effect, penalized with higher tax rates.

In 1944, in order to provide incentive for sustained management, capital gains eligibility was broadened to include growers who, after sale, still retained "an economic interest" in timber stands.[59] This provision encouraged volume-based transactions under which owners selected trees for harvest and retained others for the future.*

Other provisions of the Internal Revenue Code relating to income taxation have also benefited private forestry. For most of this century, timber growers have enjoyed favorable rules governing the deductibility of certain forest management costs. In particular, timber stand maintenance costs, such as pre-commercial thinning,** have been allowed as annual business deductions. This is an exception to the general rule of tax law that expenses contributing to an asset's value must be capitalized, in effect deferring deductions until the asset is sold. The law

---

* This change, although beneficial, was imperfect. A "retained economic interest" in timber, for example, has never been satisfactorily defined; moreover, complete liquidations of timber holdings were still rewarded if the owner could demonstrate that the timber was not held primarily for sale (*see* chapter note 58).

** Thinning is considered pre-commercial if the removed trees have little commercial value and are not sold.

makes a somewhat arbitrary distinction between such timber stand "maintenance" costs and stand "establishment" expenses, such as those for tree planting, which must be capitalized.[60]*

Even for stand establishment costs, the revenue code has been favorable, containing a generous reforestation tax credit and amortization allowance.[61] Under these provisions, expenses for reforestation up to $10,000 annually have been eligible for a 10 percent tax credit and, subject to some limitations, amortization over just seven years.

Although mitigated in recent years, the effect of estate taxation has been much more unfavorable than that of income taxation. In particular, NIPF owners and their heirs often have been faced with a significant problem: natural timber growth could cause an estate to appreciate over time to the point where, at death, premature liquidation of all or part of the stand was necessary to pay the hefty burden imposed by estate taxes. Because many NIPF owners are advanced in age and because conscientious forest management strategies may require implementation beyond the span of a single generation, such effects could be seriously disruptive to sustained forestry.[62]

Because of reform in 1976 and 1981, this is less of a problem for many landowners today. First, statutory tax credits now have the effect of exempting estates worth up to approximately $600,000 from any estate taxation.[63] Second, agricultural land, including forestland, that meets certain qualifications may be valued at its present use instead of its highest and best use for commercial or other development, and executors of such estates may extend the time available for estate tax payment under certain circumstances.[64]

The rules on estate taxation were not affected by the 1986 tax reform, but the law brought significant changes to the treatment of forestry income. Perhaps the most important

---

* When an expense is capitalized, it is added to the basis (usually determined by adjustments to the initial price) of the asset for calculation of eventual income tax liability when the asset is sold; in effect, the expense is deducted at the time of sale. For example, if a stand of timber were purchased for $100,000 and an owner spent $30,000 on new plantings, the new basis would be $130,000. If the timber sold for $150,000, the taxable profit would be $20,000 ($150,000 - $130,000), rather than $50,000 ($150,000 - $100,000).

involves capital gains. In particular, the new law repealed preferential rates for capital gains; as noted in Chapters 2 and 3, this will affect not only timber-related income but all income derived from the sale of capital assets.[65] In addition, new provisions aimed at eliminating tax shelters have complicated the eligibility criteria for a range of benefits, including the reforestation amortization and timber stand maintenance deductions.[66]*

The repeal of preferential rates for capital gains could have detrimental effects for sustained forestry. In particular, there is risk that owners now faced with a higher tax burden may forgo reforestation and other conservation measures. This was recently voiced with eloquence in a letter by C. M. Stripling, the American Forest Foundation's National Outstanding Tree Farmer for 1987:

> I finally made a sale on some trees that I've been growing half a lifetime, and the new [capital gains] tax rates are taking 71 percent more of my income than under the old rules. That's a lot of money to me. It would replace my old pickup truck. It would reforest 150 acres of land. It would more than pay for the forestry consultant I hire to make sure my forest is in good shape. The topping on this bitter cake is that the paper work required to complete the process of being fleeced has more than doubled.
>
> ...I've been planting and growing trees for more than fifty years now, and I've been through forest fires and tornados and droughts and ice storms, but the new tax laws are the biggest mess I've ever seen and the most discouraging to tree farmers. If the trend continues, we will eventually do all the work and take all the risks and then send all the money to Washington.[67]

The situation is made still more difficult by new complications with regard to management expense deductibility. In general, tax treatment of such expenses now turns on whether growers are "material" or "passive" participants in the business and whether their timber is held for sale or is considered an investment.

In particular, if timber is held for sale by a taxpayer who materially participates in the business, stand maintenance expenses will remain fully deductible.[68] However, if it is held as

---

* The reforestation tax credit was essentially unaffected by the Tax Reform Act.

an investment by a material participant, most management expenses will be allowed only to the extent that they exceed two percent of adjusted gross income.* A passive participant–*i.e.*, one who does not devote sufficient hours or demonstrate proper facts and circumstances to establish material participation–will be allowed to deduct maintenance expenses only against income from passive sources (see discussion in Chapter 2 and Appendix A).[69] Expenses in excess of these limits must be capitalized.

Sustained forestry will continue to benefit, even with these complications, from the 1986 reform's retention of the reforestation tax credit and amortization. It should also benefit form the continued deductibility of stand maintenance expenses.[70]

Nevertheless, a study conducted prior to the law's enactment by The National Friends of Grey Towers, a nonprofit organization with ties to the forestry profession, was pessimistic. It predicted that several of the reforms proposed in an early draft of the reform legislation, including the elimination of preferential rates, would lead to accelerated disposal of many industry and NIPF timberlands, a slowing or cessation of reforestation, increased pressure on public lands to boost timber harvest and soil erosion and other damage to the environment.[71] A Congressional Research Service analysis of the Tax Reform Act was more cautious in its assessment, pointing to a number of mitigating factors, but still concluded that individual timberland owners would likely pay higher taxes under the new law and that the elimination of preferential rates might reduce investments in timber management, cause a decline in the rate and quality of timber growth and reduce the long-run supply of timber.[72]

For farmers, another discouraging side effect of reform could be that sustained forestry may become a less attractive use of land than traditional rowcrop production. This could create severe environmental problems on erosion-prone lands and endanger the hundreds of thousands of acres planted with trees under Conservation Reserve Program contracts due to expire in the 1990s.

---

* Property taxes and interest remain fully deductible.

A More Realistic Approach

Federal tax policy should be revised so that it is more responsive to the economic difficulties associated with private timber management. In particular, serious consideration should be given to restoring a preferential tax rate or partial exclusion from taxable income for gains derived from the sale of timber held for 20 years or longer.

Apart from its merit as an incentive, this reform is economically justifiable given the likely effect of inflation on long-term timber management. For example, if a stand of growing timber were purchased for $100,000 and sold 20 years later for $200,000, the entire profit would be consumed by even a four percent annual rate of inflation. A preferential tax rate for timber held for decades could be considered in part as a surrogate for special rules allowing the complex calculation of the real financial gain or loss.

In addition, enactment of a preferential rate would make American policy on this issue more consistent with that of many other countries, including some with important timber resources. Australia and New Zealand assess preferential tax rates for both timber and forestland, and Finland and Norway tax timber assets favorably.[73]

Second, all material participants in timber management should be allowed to take full annual deductions for ordinary and necessary business expenses, including those pertaining to timber stand maintenance. Because of the long-term nature of timber management, the current distinction between an investor and one who holds timber as part of a trade or business is, at best, difficult to determine and presents another potential disincentive to beneficial timber investment.[74]

We do not lightly recommend policies that could be construed as a retreat from the Tax Reform Act. As noted, that statute's laudable intent was to put wage earners on a more equitable tax footing with investors and to remedy past exploitation of the tax system by those motivated more by tax shelter possibilities than by promotion of the public welfare. Certainly, given the current absence of significant federal deficit reduction attempts, we do not advocate wholesale return to pre-reform treatment of capital gains (Chapter 2).

To deter abuse of the proposed revisions for timber, emphasis should be placed on a minimum holding period of 20 years or longer for preferential rates or income exclusion.* Under no circumstances should Congress reinstate the pre-1986 requisite holding period of only six months, blatant in its encouragement of short-term, speculative timber investments.

To complement these tax changes, increased funding for NIPF assistance and education is essential. In particular, the Forest Service's State and Private Forestry programs should be expanded significantly to provide increased technical assistance to NIPF owners for sustained timber management, including assistance to owners whose acreage has been planted under the Conservation Reserve Program.[75]

Congress should also expand the Conservation Reserve with explicit direction to establish sustainable tree farming on millions of acres of marginal cropland. Such an expansion promises not only to boost private forestry but also to improve water quality while reducing crop surpluses and overall farm program spending.[76] In addition, an ambitious tree planting effort in rural America would help mitigate global warming by providing a valuable sink for atmospheric carbon dioxide.[77]

The funding necessary to strengthen and expand these programs need not inflate the federal budget deficit or come at additional taxpayer expense. Currently, the Forest Service wastes hundreds of millions of dollars annually on uneconomic, or "below-cost," sales of national forest timber that do not recover their administrative costs.[78] According to Forest Service data for Fiscal Year 1987, the timber sale programs on nearly two-thirds of the administrative units across the National Forest System lost taxpayer money.[79] If below-cost sales were eliminated or reduced, hundreds of millions of dollars could be made available to the State and Private Forestry and Forestry Incentives Programs without inflating the budget.[80]**

---

* An exception might be appropriate for stands transferred by gift or inheritance, so long as the stand is held intact for twenty years or more prior to sale.

** The presence of subsidized timber in the marketplace also provides a form of unfair competition to private growers, who must recover their costs to stay in business.

Conditions for Federal Benefits

These reforms should be accompanied by appropriate safeguards to assure that federal tax or program benefits are awarded only for environmentally sound stewardship of private forest lands. Therefore, future reforms should do for forestry what the 1986 Tax Reform Act and the 1985 Food Security Act have done for agriculture by mandating conservation accountability as a condition of federal benefits. As discussed in Chapter 3, the conservation compliance provision of the Food Security Act requires an approved conservation plan as a prerequisite to annual federal subsidies for farmers who produce crops on highly erodible land. Similarly, the Tax Reform Act allows farmers a deduction for soil and water conservation expenditures only if the expenditures are in accordance with an approved conservation plan.

Applying this concept to private forestry, all federal benefits, whether administered through the Revenue Code or direct assistance programs, should be limited to persons who are using sensible, sustained management practices. While a number of methods might accomplish such a goal, a good starting point would be to require that benefits be allowed only if land is managed in accordance with a locally approved plan providing for reforestation and incorporating protection for water quality, fish and wildlife habitat, soil and wetlands. Plans should include appropriate site-specific precautions such as protecting wildlife habitat by preserving essential snags, denning sites and mast trees in harvest areas, creating no-harvest "buffer zones" along streams and lakes to prevent water quality degradation, and restricting livestock grazing on cutover lands to protect soil and forest regeneration.[81]

With increased State and Private Forestry funding, plans could be developed with the assistance of the Cooperative Forestry program to help satisfy both owners' goals and the new conservation requirements for assistance. To assure that some minimum standards are met, site-specific plans should conform to federally-approved state forest practice guidelines to enhance production and protect environmental values. Many states already have such guidelines; others could develop them in consultation with the federal Forest Service and Environmental Protection Agency so that residents might receive federal benefits.

The concept of conditioning tax benefits on a commitment to practice sustained forestry has already been adopted in at least one state. In particular, Wisconsin's successful 1985 Forest Management Law allows preferential property taxation only on lots for which sustained forest management plans have been approved by that state's Department of Natural Resources.[82]

In addition, timber harvest plans are required under some forest practice statutes such as the California Forest Practices Act of 1973. The California plans must include a description of affected land with an explanation of the silvicultural methods to be used, the practices to be followed in order to avoid soil erosion, and any special provisions to protect unique areas.[83] Plans must be approved prior to harvest, and stocking reports must be filed to ensure adequate reforestation.[84]

In yet another approach, Washington state law segregates various logging activities into four categories according to the potential for environmental harm and establishes requirements for each. Practices with the greatest potential for harm may require an environmental impact report before logging.[85] In all, seven states had enacted comprehensive forest practice laws by early 1988, and such laws have been under formal consideration or contemplated in at least 13 more.

Although funding varies and some questions have been raised concerning the consistency of compliance, state forest practice laws are generally considered successful. A number of researchers have found that the programs significantly improve protection of both timber and amenity resources on privately owned forests. The state forestry agency in Oregon claims that the forest practice law in that state has resulted in the reforestation of 30 to 40 percent more cutover private land than would otherwise have occurred.[86]

Some have argued that compliance with these requirements is too burdensome for the small landowner.[87] However, responses to research surveys have indicated that the cost of compliance is reasonably low.[88] In California, there has been no departure from long-term timber harvest trends since the law's enactment and no evidence that owners of smaller forest tracts as a class have lowered their production as a result of stricter requirements.[89] In any event, where compliance with a forest management plan is rewarded with tax benefits or direct program assistance, financial difficulties that may be posed by the plan should be offset.

In addition to basic forest practice requirements, some mechanism should be adopted to ensure that federal incentives for private forestry do not reward short-term exploitation. For example, tax benefits for private timber production might be "recaptured" or taxed as ordinary income, if owners destructively clear their forestland. This would expand upon current Internal Revenue Service rules that enable the government, upon sales of certain property, to recapture a portion of revenues forgone through application of the reforestation tax credit and amortization. Owners who enter into cooperative agreements for direct federal program assistance might also be required to reimburse a portion or all of amounts received if the forest is cleared prematurely.* This concept also has an analogous agricultural model; under USDA's Agricultural Conservation Program, farmers who abandon multi-year agreements for cost-share assistance must reimburse the government for any assistance received.[90]

---

* As noted in Chapter 5, some states employ roll-back procedures to regain tax savings accrued to farmers who have taken advantage of preferential tax treatment of agricultural land but sell or convert the land for nonagricultural purposes.

Chapter Notes

1. USDA Forest Service, *Draft Analysis of the Timber Situation in the United States: 1989-2040* 113, 115, C-16 (1988).

2. *Id.* at C-43, C-50, C-53, C-59. Growing stock includes large diameter sawtimber trees suitable for milling lumber and smaller "poletimber" trees that may grow to sawtimber size or otherwise be commercially valuable. It does not include dead, rough and rotten trees, although a portion of these may also be salvable for commercial use. *Id.* at 122.

3. USDA, *The Private Forest-land Owners of the United States* 13-15 (Forest Service Resource Bulletin WO-1)(1982).

4. *Draft Analysis of the Timber Situation...*, *supra* note 1, at 115.

5. *Id.* at 9-25.

6. *Id.* at 7-27.

7. *Id.* at C-11, C-12, C-13.

8. USDA, *The South's Fourth Forest: Alternatives for the Future* 239-241 (Forest Resource Report No. 24)(June 1988). This estimate is slightly lower than that in earlier publications.

9. USDA Forest Service, *Draft Analysis of the Outdoor Recreational Wilderness Situation in the United States: 1989-2040* II-12 (1988).

10. *See* K. Hornback, "Social Trends and Leisure Behavior" and C. Van Doren, "Social Trends and Social Indicators," in *1985 National Outdoor Recreation Trends Symposium II* 37-47 (Department of Parks, Recreation and Tourism Management, Clemson University) (Feb. 24-27, 1985).

11. Van Doren, *supra* note 10, at 15-16.

12. C. Wilkinson and M. Anderson, "Land and Resource Planning in the National Forests," 64 *Oregon Law Review* 8-9 (1985).

13. E. Norse *et al.*, *Conserving Biological Diversity in Our National Forests* 3 (The Wilderness Society, Washington, D.C.) (June 1986).

14. *The Private Forest-Land Owners of the United States*, *supra* note 3, at 15; *Conserving Biological Diversity in Our National Forests*, *supra* note 13, at 29.

This is particularly true in light of evidence that larger private tracts are more likely to be intensively managed for timber production than smaller woodlands. *See* T. Straka *et al.*, "Size of Forest Holding and Investment Behavior of Nonindustrial Private Owners," 82 *Journal of Forestry* 495 (Aug. 1984).

15. *Draft Analysis of the Timber Situation...*, *supra* note 1, at C-9, C-12; *See also* W. Shands and R. Healy, *The Lands Nobody Wanted* 6 (Conservation Foundation, Washington, D.C.)(1977).

16. *Draft Analysis of the Timber Situation...*, *supra* note 1, at 7-27.

17. *Id.* at 145, 7-27.

18. The Wilderness Society, *Forests of the Future?* v (May 1987).

19. *Id.*

20. M. Clawson, *The Economics of U.S. Nonindustrial Private Forests* 74 (Resources For the Future)(Apr. 1974).

21. USDA, Soil Conservation Service, *Basic Statistics: 1982 National Resources Inventory* Table 38(b)(Statistical Bulletin No. 756)(Sept. 1987).

22. 16 U.S.C. §§3801-3845 (Supp. III 1985).

23. For the 1988 enrollment, USDA expanded the CRP's eligibility criteria pertaining to tree planting. Amended 7 C.F.R. §704.7(c), 53 Fed. Reg. 734.

24. USDA, Forest Service, *Report of the Forest Service, Fiscal Year 1986* 51 (Feb. 1987).

25. NRDC *et al.*, *Comments on the Proposed Land and Resource Management Plan and Draft Environmental Impact Statement for the George Washington National Forest* 44-57 (NRDC, Washington, D.C.) (Jan. 18, 1985).

26. G. Brown, *Forestry and Water Quality* 23 (Oregon State University)(1983); *Comments on the Proposed ... Plan ... for the George Washington National Forest, supra* note 25, at 45-56.

27. *"Clearcutting" Practices on the National Timberlands: Hearings Before the Subcommittee on Public Lands of the Senate Committee on Interior and Insular Affairs,* 92nd Cong., 1st Sess. 63 (Apr. 5-6, 1971)(Statement of Dr. Minckler).

28. R. Litton and P. McDonald, "Silviculture and Visual Resources," in *Town Meeting Forestry-Issues for the 1980s* 98 (Society of American Foresters)(1980).

29.   *Conserving Biological Diversity...*, *supra* note 13, at 79-90.

30.   "Clearcuts Harm Deer, Trout," *Maine Sunday Telegram* A1 (July 20, 1986).

31.   L. Minckler, *Woodland Ecology* 82-83 (1980).

32.   *Forestry and Water Quality*, *supra* note 26, at 23.

33.   G. Dunlap, "The South's Fourth Forest: Opportunities to Increase the Real Wealth of the South and the Nation," 47 *Forest Farmer* 12 (July-Aug. 1988).

34.   *See, e.g.*, Minckler, *supra* note 31; W. Smith, *Simplified Guide to Managing a Small Forest* (manuscript, Franklin, North Carolina)(June 1987).

35.   H. Glascock, Jr., "Timber Supply Concerns of Nonindustrial Private Forest Owners," in *Timber Supply: Issues and Options* at 12 (Forest Products Research Society, Madison, WI)(1979).

36.   *Id.*

37.   *Id.* at 13.

38.   C. Row, "Economies of Tract Size in Timber Growing, 76 *Journal of Forestry* 577 (Sept. 1978). *See also* F. Cubbage and T. Harris, Jr., *Tract Size and Forest Management Practices: Issues, Literature and Implications* 24 (Athens, Georgia, Agricultural Experiment Station Research Report 511)(Dec. 1986).

39.   "Size of Forest Holding and Investment Behavior of Nonindustrial Private Forest Owners," *supra* note 14, at 495.

40.   J. Royer and H. Kaiser, "Reforestation Decisions on Harvested Southern Timberlands," 81 *Journal of Forestry* 657-659 (Oct. 1983).

41.   *The Economics of U.S. Nonindustrial Private Forests*, *supra* note 20, at 31.

42.   *See, e.g.*, J. Vardaman, *Tree Farm Business Management* 23 (1978).

43.   B. Rosen, "Price Reporting of Forest Products to Nonindustrial Private Forest Land Owners," 82 *Journal of Forestry* 492-493 (Aug. 1984).

44.   C. Risbrudt *et al.*, *Forestry Incentives Program Investments in 1974: Retention Rates Through 1981* 1 (University of Minn. Station Bull. 552)(1983).

45.   R. Henly and P. Ellefson, "State-Administered Forestry Programs: Current Status and Prospects for Expansion," 5 *Renewable Resources Journal* 19, 20 (Autumn 1987).

46.   In Texas, the cost-share program is funded by private industry. Other cost-share programs are in California, Minnesota, Mississippi, North Carolina, South Carolina and Virginia. National Conference of State Legislatures, *A Legislator's Guide to Forest Resource Management* 32 (Oct. 1982).

47.   *Report of the Forest Service, Fiscal Year 1986, supra* note 24, at 42.

48.   *Id.*

49.   F. Cubbage, *Forestry Technical Assistance Programs: Research, Education, and Technology Transfer* 8-12 (Athens, Georgia)(Mar. 19, 1987).

50.   P. Hagenstein, "Incentives in Forestry - A Starting Catechism," in *The Federal Role In Providing Economic Incentives For Private Forestry* 9 (National Council on Private Forests)(Sept. 19, 1985).

51.   Cubbage, *supra* note 49, at 22.

52.   Around 11 percent of the NIPF land in the South receives some sort of technical assistance from public or private foresters, including private consultants and representatives of the forest products industry. *See* F. Cubbage and D. Hodges, "Public and Private Technical Assistance Programs for Non-industrial Private Forest Landowners in the Southern United Sates," 20 *Silva Fennica* 383 (1986).

53.   *Id.* at 21.

54.   National Association of State Foresters, *Recent Budget History 1975 - 1985 for Cooperative Forestry* (pamphlet)(undated).

55.   *USDA-Forest Service Executive Summary, FY 1987 President's Budget* 5 (Jan. 31, 1986).

56.   Cubbage, *supra* note 49, at 8.

57.   Henley and Ellefson, *supra* note 45, at 19-20; G. Meeks, Jr., "State Incentives for Nonindustrial Private Forestry," 80 *Journal of Forestry* 22 (Jan. 1982).

58.   W. Siegel and W. Ballou, Jr., "The 'Primarily for Sale' Provisions of Sections 1221 and 1231 of the Internal Revenue Code as Related to Timber Transactions," 39 *Arkansas Law Review* 75 (1985).

59.   I.R.C. §631.

60.   *See* I.R.C. §162.

61.   I.R.C. §§48(a), 194.   Stand establishment includes tree planting, direct seeding, and natural regeneration.

62.   P. Tedder and C. Sutherland, "The Federal Estate Tax: A Potential Problem for Private Nonindustrial Forest Owners in the South," *Southern Journal of Applied Forestry* 109-111 (Aug. 1979); "Timber Supply Concerns of Nonindustrial Private Forest Owners," *supra* note 35 at 12.

63.   I.R.C. §2010.

64.   I.R.C. §§2032A, 6166. The tax savings under these provisions can be significant, but the eligibility criteria are complex, designed to reward farming operations that remain within a single family for the long term and those where the farm portion constitutes most of the estate. Some critics have contended that the provisions are structured so as to benefit large, corporate-style operations more than the smaller "family farms" they were intended to help. *See* M. Caughlin and J. Noble, "Implications of Federal Tax Provisions for Agricultural Land Availability," in *Agricultural Land Availability* 475, 483-485 (Senate Agriculture Committee Print)(July 1981).

65.   The Tax Reform Act retained the statutory definition of capital assets, including that pertaining specifically to timber, while setting the tax rate equal to that for ordinary income.   Tax Reform Act of 1986, Pub. L. No. 99-514, §301, 100 Stat. 2085, 2216-2219 (1986) [hereafter TRA] (amending I.R.C. §1202); I.R.C. §631.

66.   *See, e.g.*, TRA §§501, 511 (adding I.R.C. §469 and amending I.R.C. §163).

67.   C. Stripling, "Capital Gains Aren't Just for the Rich," *The Washington Post* A23 (Mar. 26, 1988).

68.   W. Siegel, "Implications of the 1986 Federal Tax Reform Act for Forestry," in *Proceedings of the 1986 Society of American Foresters National Convention* 257 (Birmingham, Alabama) (Oct. 1986).

69.   *Id.*

70.   F. Benfield *et al.*, "Conservation Gains in the Tax Reform Act," 11 *Harvard Environmental Law Review* 415, 427-29 (1987).

71.   H. Canham and J. Gray, Eds., *Federal Income Tax Change and the Private Forest Sector* i-ii (1986); *see also* R. Sedjo *et al.*, *Tax Reform and Timber Supply* (Resources for the Future)(1986).

72.   R. Gorte and J. Taylor, *Timber Industry: Possible Effects of Various Tax Reform Proposals* 6, 7 (Congressional Research Service Issue Brief No. IB86009)(Dec. 1, 1986). As to mitigating factors, the authors suggest that any decline in timber supply as a result of tax reform might cause higher prices and thus some re-stimulation of timber investment. They also note that factors unrelated to timber income taxation, including wood products markets and NIPF owner priorities, could have greater impacts on timber management than the Tax Reform Act.

73.   Arthur Andersen & Company, *Taxation of Timber and Forest Land in Selected Countries with Important Timber Resources* 4, 9, 32, 75, 81 (Oct. 3, 1985).

74.   *See* "The 'Primarily for Sale' Provisions of Sections 1221 and 1231...," *supra* note 58, at 78-97.

75.   *See* Memorandum of Milton Hertz, ASCS Administrator *et al.*, to State and County Executive Directors, Re: Conservation Reserve Tree Planting (June 16, 1987).

76.   *See* S. Nunn, "Agricultural Policy: Ripe for Reform," 4 *Issues in Science and Technology* 56-59 (1988).

77.   *See* D. Dudek, "Offsetting New CO_2 Emissions," (Environmental Defense Fund)(Sept. 1988); W. Sullivan, "Forests Sought to Counter Greenhouse Effect," *The New York Times* C4 (Sept. 20, 1988).

78.   *See e.g.*, G. Helfand *et al.*, "Reform of Uneconomic Federal Timber Sale Procedures is Badly Needed and Long Overdue," Testimony of the Natural Resources Defense Council before the Subcommittee on Public Lands and the Subcommittee on General Oversight, Northwest Power and Forest Management, House Committee on Interior and Insular Affairs (June 11, 1985).

79.   *See* USDA Forest Service, "Timber Sale Program Annual Report, FY 1987 Test, Forest Level Information," (1987).

80.   For an interesting elaboration on this subject, *see* U.S. Rep. J. Jontz, "Government and Public Programs: The Challenge to Using Forests for Economic and Social Development," (paper presented at the Annual Meeting of the Society of American Foresters, Minneapolis, Minnesota)(Oct. 19, 1987).

81.   USDA, Forest Service, *Land and Resource Management Plan: Green Mountain National Forest* 4.19, 4.31 (1986); National Wildlife Federation, *Assessment of the Weyerhaeuser Company's Forestry Operations in Southwestern Arkansas and Southeastern Oklahoma* 8 (Report of the Blue-Ribbon Panel on Wildlife and Forestry)(Oct. 1982).

82.   G. Stoddard, "Integrated Resource Management and Private Forestry: One State's Approach," 86 *Journal of Forestry* (Feb. 1988).

83.   P. Ellefson and F. Cubbage, *State Forest Practice Laws and Regulations: A Review and Case Study for Minnesota* 12, 13 (University of Minnesota Agricultural Experiment Station Bulletin 536-1980)(Forestry Series 32)(undated).

84.   *Id.*

85.   *Id.* at 13-15.

86.   For an elaboration of forest practice laws in Alaska, California, Idaho, Massachusetts, Nevada, Oregon and Washington, *see* R. Henly, P. Ellefson and R. Moulton, "State Regulation of Private Forest Practices: What Accomplishments at What Costs?" 13 *Western Wildlands* 23-28 (Winter 1988).

87.   *State Forest Practice Laws and Regulations..., supra* note 83, at 26.

88.   "State Regulation of Private Forest Practices...," *supra* note 86, at 24, 27.

89.   Harvest volumes in California have been declining steadily since 1953, showing no shift attributable to the 1973 law. The most likely explanation for harvest decline is the liquidation of the state's stocks of high volume old-growth timber stands.   Notwithstanding some general decline in harvest volume, employment in the California forest products industry rose steadily from about 81,000 in 1965 to more than one million in 1979, a relatively good year for the industry.   F. Ruderman, *Production, Prices, Employment and Trade in the Northwest Forest Industries* 16 (PNW Forest and Range Experiment Station)(1980); C. Bolsinger, *California Forests: Trends, Problems and Opportunities* 72 (PNW Forest and Range Experiment Station Resource Bulletin PNW-89). Some have speculated that harvest decreases in California may be due to new state tax laws that allow owners to hold timber for longer periods of time without paying excessive taxes based on the volume of standing timber.   Letter from J. Ronald, Leader, Cooperative Forest Management, to C. Corkery, NRDC (Forest Service, Pacific Southwest Region)(Nov. 20, 1987).

90.   Telephone conversation with James R. McMullen, Director, Conservation and Environmental Protection, USDA Agricultural Stabilization and Conservation Service (Dec. 9, 1987).

8

Conclusion–A Tax Agenda for Conservation

American agriculture is at a crossroads. Its present path is perilous for rural America's natural resource base and, ultimately, for the people our farms employ and feed. A more sustainable path will, on the other hand, foster long term world food security and a healthy rural environment.

Public policy will be a major determinant of which path is taken. In the coming years, deliberations on sustainable agriculture will intensify in the halls of Congress, at the U.S. Department of Agriculture and in state legislatures.

This book has sought to bring an important, and largely overlooked subject–tax policy–into those deliberations. As Chapters 2 and 3 elaborate, inattention to Revenue Code concerns has a history of seriously undercutting conservation programs. A failure to learn from past mistakes would be a gross disservice to this nation's farmers and consumers.

In the foregoing chapters, we have made a variety of recommendations for needed reforms. In this endeavor, we do not claim to have all the answers. Certainly, we are well aware that many of the concepts presented need further discussion and refinement. Our hope is to stimulate just that.

Our recommendations can be summarized in four general categories. First, Congress should eliminate hidden tax subsidies that reward unsustainable agriculture. This means limiting deductions for fertilizer expenses to efficient applications as well as restricting access to cash accounting and accelerated depreciation to just those farmers who sensibly protect the environment. It also means repealing the water depletion allowance and ending special breaks for paving prime farmland.

Second, Congress must resist political pressure to reinstate tax shelters that have rewarded unsustainable agriculture and exacerbated the federal deficit. This means preserving the repeal of the capital gains exclusion, investment tax credit and land clearing deduction. It also means retaining new limitations governing passive investment losses, soil and water conservation expenses and cash accounting.

Third, the federal government should use tax policy, where appropriate, as a reasonable inducement to sustainable agriculture. The charitable contribution deduction for conservation easements has enormous untapped potential for improving the quality of the rural environment. A modest excise tax on pesticides and fertilizers would be an excellent way to raise revenue for needed research and education on low-chemical farming systems. Because of its extraordinary economic difficulties, sustained tree farming on private woodlands merits specialized tax treatment.

Fourth, the federal government and the states should provide complementary forms of assistance where tax and market considerations provide insufficient leverage for agricultural conservation. To supplement differential property tax assessments for farmland protection, states should look to mechanisms such as sensible land use planning and purchase of development rights. The federal government should supplement charitable contribution deductions for conservation easements with more direct acquisition techniques and the use of easements to forgive delinquent farm debt. Public assistance programs for nonindustrial private forestry should be strengthened.

Of course, tax reform is just one piece of the puzzle. Indeed, there is much to be said for a neutral tax code that leaves policy choices to more direct substantive enactments. The sustainable agriculture agenda must address shortcomings in federal commodity support programs, pesticide regulation and food safety, groundwater protection, control of farmland runoff pollution, water pricing policies, research and education. In the meantime, however, Congress at least should ensure that the tax code's complex system of incentives and sanctions is consistent with the county's compelling conservation needs.

The stakes are high, and the tasks ahead are daunting. Our outlook is buoyed, however, by recent major progress in agricultural conservation and tax reform, particularly the historic natural resource provisions within the Food Security and Tax

Reform Acts. There is much encouragement to be found in these developments, and we conclude in the hope that the conservation momentum that has manifested itself of late will eventually lead to fully enlightened policies for sustainable agriculture.

Appendix A:
Passive Investment Loss Limitations

To remove certain tax shelter opportunities, the 1986 Tax Reform Act specified that deductions associated with business activities in which the taxpayer does not "materially participate" may be claimed only to the extent that they do not exceed income from passive sources. For example, assume that a physician's principal income derives from a full-time medical practice augmented by income from investments in a farm and rental apartments. The physician plays no active role in managing the farm or the rental units. This individual realizes a net annual loss of $12,000 in the farm and a net profit of $9,000 in the rental investment. Under new section 469 of the Internal Revenue Code, only $9,000 of the farming loss can be deducted; the remaining $3,000 of the loss cannot be used to reduce taxable income from the medical practice.

The language of the Tax Reform Act is unclear as to what constitutes "material participation." Nevertheless, the statute's legislative history sheds some light on this issue. The Senate Finance Committee suggested that the definition generally will be met by "an individual who does not perform physical work relating to a farm, but who is treated as having self-employment income with respect to the farm."[1] Thus, individuals apparently may satisfy the test by making management decisions even though they do not themselves carry out the farming operations. The Committee emphasized, however, that the participation must be more than "merely formal and nominal," noting that "[i]f the management decisions being made by the taxpayer are illusory (*e.g.*, whether to feed the cattle or let them starve), or guided by an expert in the absence of any independent exercise of judgment by the taxpayer, or unimportant to the business, they are given little weight."[2]

Complex regulations recently proposed by the Internal Revenue Service specify seven tests by which taxpayers may

---

[1] S. Rep. No. 313, 99th Cong., 2d Sess. 733, 734 (May 29, 1986).

[2] *Id.* at 734.

establish material participation with respect to the passive loss rules and thus qualify for full deductions. Most of these tests contemplate a minimum threshold of time devoted to the source of income. For example, someone may qualify by spending more than 500 hours in the activity during the relevant tax year. In addition, taxpayers may qualify by spending just 100 hours in farming operations provided they can demonstrate sufficient "facts and circumstances" to support their case.[3]

---

[3] 26 C.F.R. §§1.469-5T, 53 Fed. Reg. 5725-5728.

Appendix B:
Depreciation of Capital Investments

In a discussion of capital investments, the Internal Revenue Service's *Farmer's Tax Guide* advises, "In general, if you buy a farm property, such as machinery, equipment, or buildings, that has a useful life of more than a year, you cannot deduct its entire cost in one year. Instead, you must spread the cost over more than one year and deduct a part of it each year. For most types of property, this is called 'depreciation.'"[1] Depreciation of capital investments is vitally important to American agriculture, one of the nation's most capital-intensive industries. Without dwelling on the complexities of federal tax rules, the following discussion examines the basic depreciation opportunities available to agricultural taxpayers.

The Accelerated Cost Recovery System (ACRS)

The Tax Reform Act of 1986 retained a modified version of the "Accelerated Cost Recovery System" (ACRS),[2] available to taxpayers since 1981 when Congress enacted a set of tax reforms intended to stimulate business investment. In brief, accelerated cost recovery permits the full depreciation of any eligible investment property over a period shorter than the property's useful life. Most pieces of farm machinery and equipment placed in service after December 31, 1986 are now assigned to a "recovery class" in which depreciation deductions are staged over seven years.[3] Various land improvements, including drainage facilities, fall into a 15-year recovery class.[4]

---

[1] U.S. Department of the Treasury, Internal Revenue Service, *Farmer's Tax Guide* 26 (IRS Publication 225) (Oct. 1986).

[2] Tax Reform Act of 1986, Pub. L. No. 99-514, §201, 100 Stat. 2085, 2121-2142 (amending I.R.C. §§167, 168) (Oct. 22, 1986) [hereinafter TRA].

[3] *Farmer's Tax Guide, supra* note 1, at 31.

[4] U.S. Department of Treasury, Internal Revenue Service, *Depreciation* 5 (I.R.S. Publication 534) (Dec. 1987).

Within the accelerated recovery schedules, a farmer or other investor has two basic options. First, a taxpayer using ACRS may depreciate any qualifying investment using a "straight line" procedure whereby deductions are taken in equal annual increments over the length of the recovery period.[5] Alternatively, and preferably for most agricultural taxpayers, annual writeoffs for land improvements, as well as most farm machinery and equipment can be calculated by a 150 percent declining balance method whereby deductions begin at one and one-half times the initial allowance under a straight line formulation.[6]

Table 1 in Chapter 3 illustrates the application of straight line and 150 percent declining balance alternatives to the ACRS depreciation of a $90,000 combine. An adjustment is made to account for the fact that most investment property is purchased and placed into service in the middle of the tax year. Typically, as in the example, the Internal Revenue Service invokes a "half-year convention," in which depreciable property automatically is treated as having been placed in service at the mid-point of its initial tax year. Thus the ACRS deduction in year one is halved, and the taxpayer may claim a similar partial-year deduction in year 8. Internal Revenue Service rules allow a taxpayer who opts for the 150 percent declining balance method to maximize tax savings by switching in year four to straight line calculations for the remainder of the investment.[7]

"Section 179" Expense Deductions

For depreciable investments placed in service after December 31, 1986 and qualifying as Section 38 property,[8] Section 179 of

[5] *Id.* at 18, 19.

[6] Prior to technical corrections legislation enacted in 1988, most investment property in the seven year recovery class could be depreciated under an even more accelerated "double declining" balance method whereby first year deductions began at twice the comparable straight line level.

[7] *See Depreciation, supra* note 4, at 6.

[8] Section 38 property includes tangible personal property (farm machinery and
(continued...)

the revenue code permits an expense deduction of up to $10,000 of the purchase price, provided total business investments during the tax year do not exceed $200,000.[9] Where a taxpayer's total investments exceed $200,000, the maximum amount eligible for section 179 expensing is reduced by one dollar for each investment dollar over $200,000. Therefore, the provision cannot be used to advantage by taxpayers with total annual investments exceeding $210,000; it acts as an incentive for only limited investment.

Nevertheless, many investors benefit from using section 179 expensing in tandem with the ACRS. The provision essentially enables further hastening of the cost recovery process by greater "front-loading" of deductions for capital expenditures. In the first year of the ACRS schedules for the $90,000 combine illustrated in Table 1 in Chapter 3, the investor elects to claim $10,000 as a section 179 expense and simultaneously initiates the 150 percent declining balance or straight line method for depreciating the $80,000 remainder.

---

[8](...continued)
equipment meet this test), other tangible property (not including a building or structural component) that is used as an integral part of production (certain land improvements such as drainage systems meet this test) and single-purpose agricultural or horticultural buildings.

[9] I.R.C. §179, as amended by TRA §202. The TRA raised the allowable section 179 deduction from $5,000 to $10,000, thus compensating somewhat for the repeal of the regular 10 percent Investment Tax Credit.

Appendix C:
The Limited Reach of the Food Security Act

Farm program participation is largely a function of fluctuations in agricultural market conditions. Participation rates in 1987 exceeded 80 percent for all basic program crops (wheat, corn, oats, grain sorghum, barley, cotton and rice).[1] This reflects both the attractiveness of recent program terms and the perils of today's rural economy, in which unassisted commodity prices are frequently too low to allow profit from simple market sale of farm products. However, if history provides a true indication of future trends, farm program participation—and hence the strength of the sodbuster and swampbuster provisions—will diminish should the current depressed conditions in rural America abate.[2]

Such a scenario might well result from an increase in export demand for U.S. farm commodities. Although this nation's share of global agricultural markets has been in a tailspin throughout the 1980s and may never regain its former prominence, some developments may signal a turnabout. In particular, a major wheat sale to the Soviet Union was announced by USDA in the spring of 1987.[3] This sale and others made subsequently were reminiscent of international grain deals in the 1970s that triggered short-term farm prosperity but also "fencerow-to-fencerow" plowing of marginal cropland across the country.

Reductions in federal spending on USDA farm programs also could lessen the impact of sodbuster and swampbuster sanctions. Although Congress appears unprepared to adopt a wholesale retrenchment of government intervention in agriculture, public sentiment is growing for mitigating the escalating cost of farm programs. Already, many large farming operations have little incentive to participate in federal assistance programs because of

---

[1] USDA News Release, "Producers Enroll 194.5 of 231.7 Million Acreage Bases in 1987 Farm Programs," (Apr. 28, 1987).

[2] R. Heimlich and L. Langer, *Swampbusting: Wetland Conversion and Farm Programs* 25 (USDA-ERS Agricultural Economic Report No. 551) (Aug. 1986).

[3] W. Sinclair, "Soviets Agree to Buy Subsidized U.S. Wheat," *The Washington Post* A1 (May 1, 1987).

a legally mandated $50,000 per producer cap on subsidy payments.

The Food Security Act's sodbuster and swampbuster provisions could themselves prove barriers to farm program participation. In cases where the expense of developing an erosion control system or the forgone income opportunities associated with land conversion exceed program benefits, farmers have virtually no financial motivation to participate.[4]

Among the potential croplands most vulnerable to plowing under such scenarios are the highly erodible fields enrolled in the Food Security Act's landmark Conservation Reserve Program, which compensates farmers for placing severely eroding cropland under 10-year contracts that require the establishment of soil-saving perennial grass or tree cover.[5] More than 23 million acres had been accepted into the program by mid-1987; the federal contract payments on these acres alone will reach $12 billion over ten years.[6] USDA has made additional significant outlays in covering half the cost of establishing protective vegetation cover and in awarding special inducements such as a corn bonus during the signup period for the program held in March 1987.[7] A return of these lands to the cropland base after contracts expire would seriously compromise the basic purpose of this major investment of a permanent transition to more sustainable uses of lands that do not belong in intensive crop production.

---

[4] See S. Batie, "Conservation Cross Compliance: An Alternative Perspective," (Paper delivered to USDA Agricultural Outlook Conference) (Dec. 3, 1986).

[5] Food Security Act of 1985, Pub. L. No. 99-198, Title XII, 99 Stat. 1354, 1504-1518, 16 U.S.C. §3801 et seq.

[6] Telephone conversation with Jim Canavan, USDA Forest Service (Aug. 18, 1987).

[7] See USDA, FY 1986 Annual Report, Conservation Reserve Program (Jan. 5, 1987); "USDA Accepts Over Ten Million More Acres in Conservation Reserve," (USDA Office of Information News Release) (Mar. 13, 1987).